# DEL BOSQUE, EMERY, BENITEZ & LUIS ENRIQUE

## Practices and Training Sessions

**Published by**

# DEL BOSQUE, EMERY, BENITEZ & LUIS ENRIQUE

## Practices and Training Sessions

**First Published April 2019 by SoccerTutor.com**
**info@soccertutor.com | www.SoccerTutor.com**

**UK:** 0208 1234 007 | **US:** (305) 767 4443 | **ROTW:** +44 208 1234 007
**ISBN:** 978-1-910491-30-0

**Edited by** Alex Fitzgerald - SoccerTutor.com

**Cover Design by** Alex Macrides, Think Out Of The Box Ltd.
Email: design@thinkootb.com Tel: +44 (0) 208 144 3550

### Diagrams

Diagram designs by SoccerTutor.com. All the diagrams in this book have been created using SoccerTutor.com Tactics Manager Software available from www.SoccerTutor.com

Note: While every effort has been made to ensure the technical accuracy of the content of this book, neither the author nor publishers can accept any responsibility for any injury or loss sustained as a result of the use of this material.

# CONTENTS

# UNAI EMERY ....................................................38

# RAFAEL BENÍTEZ ..............................................................76

# LUIS ENRIQUE ..............................................................95

# DIAGRAM KEY

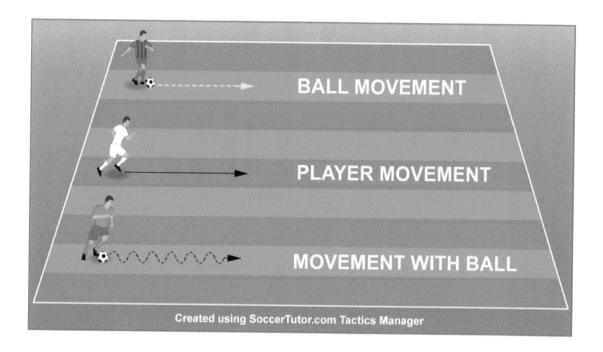

BALL MOVEMENT

PLAYER MOVEMENT

MOVEMENT WITH BALL

Created using SoccerTutor.com Tactics Manager

# PRACTICE FORMAT

**Each practice includes clear diagrams with supporting training notes such as:**

- Name / Objective of Practice
- Description of Practice
- Variation or Progression (if applicable)
- Coaching Points (if applicable)

*Del Bosque, Emery, Benítez & Luis Enrique*

# VICENTE DEL BOSQUE

**This section includes:**

- Vicente Del Bosque Interview
- 2 Real Madrid Passing Practices
- 4 Full Real Madrid Training Sessions (14 Practices)

*Del Bosque, Emery, Benítez & Luis Enrique*

# VICENTE DEL BOSQUE

*"I don't just want to be the coach who wins, but the coach who educates."*

## Coaching Roles

- **Spain**
  (2008 - 2016)
- **Besiktas**
  (2004 - 2005)
- **Real Madrid**
  (1999 - 2003)

## Honours

- **FIFA World Cup**
  (2010)
- **UEFA European Championship**
  (2012)
- **UEFA Champions League**
  (2000, 2002)
- **La Liga**
  (2001, 2003)
- **FIFA World Coach of the Year**
  (2012)
- **UEFA Club Coach of the Year**
  (2002)

## Most Used Formations

- **4-3-3, 4-2-3-1, 4-1-4-1 & 4–6–0 (False 9)**

## Style of Play

"Each coach has what we think is the most ideal way of playing, but we must also be flexible."

"I like for a team not to worry too much about the result, to play freely, to not back down, be a team that develops the game, have depth and have a good balance between the short game and the long game."

## Coaching Philosophy

"Be careful, you have an idea, a style, and then you should observe the players you have, because you will give them the best outline and instructions based on the quality of the model."

"I am not in favour of overwhelming the player with too much information, as I think instructions should be very concise and concrete and should not be too complicated."

"During each practice, the coach should be more reflective and should try to reach the player, not only by instructing him, but also trying to educate the player."

"I believe more in the global exercise (integrated training), in which the player does everything at the highest speed possible."

## What it takes to be a Successful Coach

"In leadership, you must be likeable, affable, cordial, and above all emotional. The fashion of authoritarian leadership is gone. Football is about life. You can't be angry all day."

"Success without honour is the greatest failure."

# VICENTE DEL BOSQUE

## Interview with Vicente Del Bosque

# INTERVIEW WITH VICENTE DEL BOSQUE

**SOURCE:** Vicente Del Bosque interview conducted by Paco Cordobés and published by **abfutbol.es**

### Do we always have to maintain our personal style as a coach or do we have to adapt to the players?

**Vicente Del Bosque:** "In principle, you have to see the characteristics of your team, of your players, but we must also take into account other circumstances. When I was at Real Madrid, I tried not to move away from the history of the club, its trajectory. There have been specific moments at Real Madrid when some coaches wanted to mark their own style, but I think that a coach must be faithful to the club's history, and at the same time, not deviate from the characteristics of the club's players, but instead enhance these signs of identity with the quality of the model."

### To face a game, would you always use the same system or study the opposition and adapt to different circumstances?

**VDB:** "Each coach has what we think is the most ideal way of playing, but we must also be flexible. I believe that in my time at Real Madrid I have demonstrated my flexibility well. During our run to winning the Champions League in 2000, we changed our system of play. We had been using a back 4 all season and when we played Manchester United in the quarter finals, we used a defence with 3 centre backs and won with a team that were not given a chance. We knew what we wanted, what we wanted at that moment, and we adapted to a very specific situation. We played like this until the final against Valencia, using **Karanca**, **Hierro** (or Helguera) and **Iván Campo** as our centre backs."

(See 3-5-2 image below)

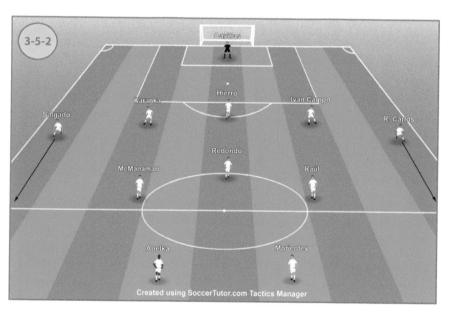

Created using SoccerTutor.com Tactics Manager

Vicente Del Bosque showed his flexibility by switching to play with 3 centre backs in a 5-3-2.

Real Madrid first used this system of play against Manchester Utd in the quarter final of the Champions League (2000) and played this way through to the final, which they won.

**Source:** Vicente Del Bosque interview conducted by Paco Cordobés and published by **abfutbol.es**

**VDB:** "We tried to find a stable system for Real Madrid, but then with the subsequent arrivals of **Makélélé** and **Figo**, and then **Zidane**, other situations arose, so we had to adapt to the new situation. Some said we should play with one defensive midfielder and others said we should play with two. We had to adapt to a very unusual situation within the team and we looked for the best solution. And that is what everyone should understand, look for the ideal, but then you have to be flexible for different situations, while always maintaining the quality of your model."

The following 3 diagrams show the tactical work of Vicente Del Bosque during his time as Real Madrid Head Coach. With the arrival of new signings, the team had to adapt to the special technical characteristics of these players. There was always flexibility in the system and their great success on the pitch shows that the team always benefited.

## Del Bosque's 4-3-3 Real Madrid Formation with 1 Defensive Midfielder

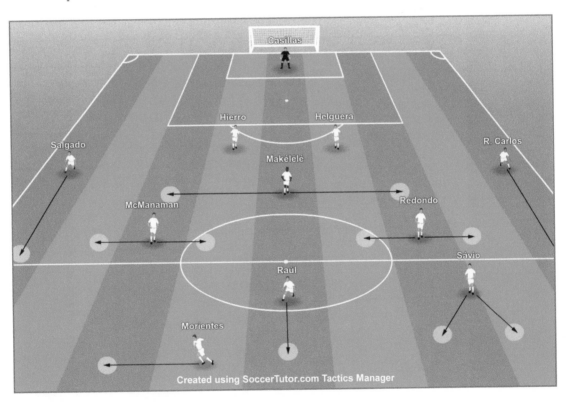

Created using SoccerTutor.com Tactics Manager

**Makélélé** played as the only defensive midfielder and covered both sides, depending on the positioning of the full backs at the time. **McManaman** and **Redondo** played as conventional central midfielders within a 4-3-3 system. **Sávio** played a creative role, always trying to receive in between the lines. He was often helped by the advanced overlapping runs of the left back **Roberto Carlos**.

**Morientes** would often move wide to provide a passing option and **Raúl** would move into the centre forward's position.

**Source:** Vicente Del Bosque interview conducted by Paco Cordobés and published by **abfutbol.es**

## Del Bosque's 4-2-3-1 Real Madrid Formation with 2 Defensive Midfielders

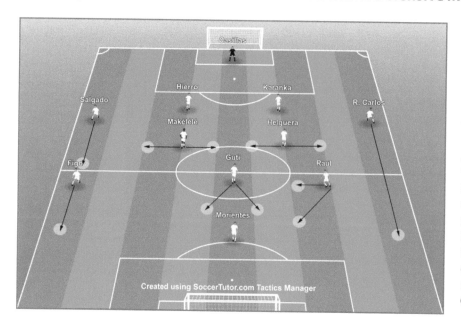

With **Makélélé** and **Helguera** both playing as defensive midfielders, Del Bosque was able to play 3 attacking players (**Figo**, **Guti** and **Raúl**) behind the centre forward **Morientes**. **Raúl** would often move inside and be helped by the advanced overlapping runs of **Roberto Carlos**.

## Del Bosque's 4-1-4-1 Real Madrid Formation with 1 Defensive Midfielder

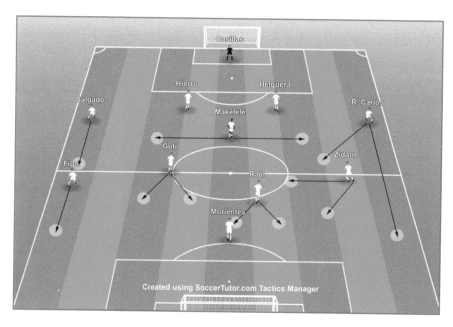

Once **Zidane** arrived as the team's playmaker, Del Bosque played a more attacking formation (with 1 defensive midfielder) based on dominating possession with expansive football.

**Zidane** would often move inside and be helped by the advanced overlapping runs of **Roberto Carlos**.

**Source:** Vicente Del Bosque interview conducted by Paco Cordobés and published by **abfutbol.es**

### Do you consider that a coach should be adaptable throughout the season in general?

**VDB:** "I believe that each match is unique, each team is different. Of course you have to take the opposition into account.

We cannot say: "We are like this and we have to play like this." Each opponent has its virtues and we must accept them."

### What do you think of observing and analysing your opponents? It seems more and more coaches focus a lot of their time on this, is this positive?

**VDB:** "I think all the data has to be analysed to find out what is relevant. Analysis is important and what is found to be substantial must be transmitted to the players."

### Do you think that the coach should influence the philosophy of a club or team if they believe it not to be adequate?

**VDB:** "Each club has its history and its own philosophy. One thing is the game system that each coach will use depending on the players they have and another is the style of play that has traditionally been used at a club. I do know what my style is within a team, regardless of the tactical model you should use by club tradition.

I like for a team not to worry too much about the result, to play freely, to not back down, be a team that develops the game, have depth and have a good balance between the short game and the long game. That is the style of Real Madrid, always taking the initiative, and this clearly agreed with my style of play in this case. Be careful, this is an idea, a style, and then you should observe the players you have, because you will give them the best outline and instructions based on the quality of the model."

### Do you trust tactical discipline more or do you prefer to follow the creativity of a player?

**VDB:** "You cannot be absolute in anything. During my time in Madrid we were often accused of not having a game system, that there was no work being done. In the team there was a freedom for the player, of course, but there was also something in which the player was supported, there are some rules and a team, there are some automatisms that are created with the training we do day to day, which are very critical but people do not see it.

I believe that a team that wants to be a champion, and in my case, that has been a champion in Spain, has to base itself on something, on a set of rules. You cannot just rely on the creativity of great individuals, as you need a mix. The balance between the individuals and the collective work is what brings success. If this balance does not exist, it is impossible."

### What should a coach never do?

**VDB:** "A coach is not just the tactical part, because there is a development of the whole strategy with many parts. Some coaches have the ability to manage a training model and others do not use a model, but instead use a more flexible training system. Either way, the strategy that you are going to follow must work in parallel with the development of the action. You decide the game system, the players, the training you will do the next day - this is everything in the development of the whole strategy.

I am not a supporter of simply instructing players, as I think this misuses practices. The coach should not be angry all day to try to influence the player to respond and appear to be aggressive until he sees what he deems to be correct. During each practice, the coach should be more reflective and should try to reach the player, not only by instructing him, but also trying to educate the player."

**Source:** Vicente Del Bosque interview conducted by Paco Cordobés and published by **abfutbol.es**

**Since you have been at Real Madrid, you have marked your own style which may have influenced other coaches. Many of us have realised that sometimes silence instead of aggression from the bench can be beneficial...**

**VDB:** "Those cries are often to hurt the player and have no clear purpose. Most of the time more is achieved by reasoning than with aggression, but each coach has their own style. I believe that with education, a player is more receptive. It's like when training kids. For example, if a player has failed to score a chance, it is not a good idea to ask "How can you not score that?" - You should instead explain why the player did not score. For instance, explain that they should have used the inside of their foot for a larger surface area, rather than the instep. You can fail, but you have to tell the child why he failed, in case he failed for something that was not well executed. The parents must also do it, to aid the education."

**Bombarding the player with instructions, in training, in team talks ... is it positive to continuously send information to the player, even minutes before a match? Or can excessive information hurt the player?**

**VDB:** "I am not in favour of overwhelming the player with too much information, I think instructions should be very concise and concrete and should not be too complicated. Before a game or during halftime of a game, you have to be extraordinarily concrete and that can be very fruitful. You don't want to make the players dizzy and if your talk goes on and on, this causes the players to disperse. For that reason, I believe that it is necessary to be very precise so that the players can handle and absorb all the information."

**Is the work before a match all done during the week and left for the players' reflection or do you think it is positive to continue working on match day?**

**VDB:** "Normally at the beginning of the season or preseason, the foundations of the team are set and come to fruition during the season. Most of the training during the season is low intensity due to the busy schedule, so the majority of the high intensity training is done during matches.

Real Madrid play every 3 days so it is difficult, in training to learn new habits that you did not acquire at the beginning of the season, and that you are using to get through the matches. You play on Sunday. On Monday you recover, on Tuesday you prepare for the next game (Wednesday) and you can introduce some new instructions but you cannot change too much. It is also true that prior to the matches you have to give the touch to that match, but generally the season long habits must be clear."

**If you had to describe the professional coach, what would you highlight?**

**VDB:** "Well, many aspects that you acquire. You must be accompanied properly, you do not need to be an expert in physical preparation, because you already have a fitness coach, who is a specialist and those specialists are there to support you. But at the same time, you have to control everything, that is, you are not a specialist in physical preparation but you have knowledge of this work and you must control all of that.

You don't only choose the players, you don't only develop the strategy and create a pleasant work environment, you are also a representation of the club - the coach is the image of the club worldwide and that representation must be correct, because it is representing an entity, in my case, Real Madrid. You have to know how to handle press conferences very well; the press conferences are routine, but there are times when the press conferences must be use to send a specific message. There is not just one thing, it's a very big job with many different aspects to it and the more things you master, the better coach you will be."

---

**Source:** Vicente Del Bosque interview conducted by Paco Cordobés and published by **abfutbol.es**

*Del Bosque, Emery, Benítez & Luis Enrique*

### What is the image that a coach should transmit to his players as a person?

**VDB:** "For a balanced, sensible person, do not give the impression that you know a lot, but not that you know little, do not give the impression that your figure is fundamental, give respect, do not go to the locker room as if you were the owner."

### As the world of football is being modernised, many more people accompany the Head Coach. To what extent is this beneficial or harmful to the world of football?

**VDB:** "If it's true that football should not lose its nature of what the game is, but you also have to have or try to support yourself from the most advanced means to control more things. For example, people subjectively told us that **Makélélé** lost a lot of balls, but our data showed that he only lost 5% of the balls. Here we can clearly see that the opinions do not coincide with the reality, because the data we have does not agree with what people think, so that data should serve to value them.

If a player in central midfield intervenes 80 or 90 times throughout a match, we know that it this is the correct participation and if we see that he participates 35 times, we think, that this player is not doing the work that the team needs. I do not say that I am in favour or against being more and more scientific, but it is true that we have to rely on data."

### Does the coach really have to focus on what interests him, which is technique and tactics?

**VDB:** "The coach has to control everything, but you should not interfere with peoples' specialist jobs. You can know about diet or nutrition and that is good, but you should not intervene. It is not the job of the coach to tell players what they should or shouldn't eat, because this is the role of the nutritionist and doctor. They are experts and have plans for each specific player.

When it comes to physical preparation, the fitness coaches are physical football coaches so you will work closely with them to produce training drills and sessions."

### Does a coach have to specialise in psychology?

**VDB:** "I tell you what I have done, we have moved through the experience and the balance that I have had in my life as a player, but then I have seen the theoretical things of prepared people, experts in psychology and I saw that they were not far from what we have done. That is a fact.

In some cases, it will be indicated that a specialist in psychology intervenes and perhaps in other cases not. The one who commands in the dressing room is the figure of the coach."

### Integrated training (global) or analytical training (individual)?

**VDB:** "Integrated training, but the analytical (specific/isolated training) cannot be discarded altogether when it comes to the individual improvement of a player in certain actions.

Analytical training is logical, but I believe that there is less benefit obtained from analytical training compared to integrated training. I think it has little transference. I believe more in the global exercise (integrated training), in which the player does everything at the highest speed possible."

### Do you attach the physical work to the technical-tactical work?

**VDB:** "Well, yes, why not. However, what happens is that there are training drills that no matter how much we want to integrate them into technique and tactics, there are elements of physical preparation that are impossible to integrate, of course."

---

**Source:** Vicente Del Bosque interview conducted by Paco Cordobés and published by **abfutbol.es**

**Today, games are played every 3 or 4 days. What percentage of importance would you give to training and recovery respectively?**

**VDB:** "Right now the matches mark a lot of training, it marks everything. If you play 9 games in a month, it is impossible for you to train at high intensity. Usually, medium intensity or low intensity training is needed, so you have to be very careful. It is not about training too little or too much, but exactly what the players need."

**Is there a year training plan or does it depend what is happening in the competitions during the season?**

**VDB:** "You have to mark a line of work throughout the year and right now, according to football and I'm talking about what I know, you cannot say that in January I want to be very strong and in March too. I believe that now there is a tendency towards stability from the beginning of the season until the end of the season, which is nine months that we have to be at a high point of preparation."

**What basic condition must there be when training children or professionals?**

**VDB:** "It has to be varied, enjoyable, and everything you do has to transfer to the competition. You have to try to get closer to the reality of the game. Everything that does not come close to reality will mean that you are doing a false training."

---

**Source:** Vicente Del Bosque interview conducted by Paco Cordobés and published by **abfutbol.es**

*Del Bosque, Emery, Benítez & Luis Enrique*

# VICENTE DEL BOSQUE

## Real Madrid Passing Drills

*Del Bosque, Emery, Benítez & Luis Enrique*

# 1. Passing Square: Short and Long Support Play

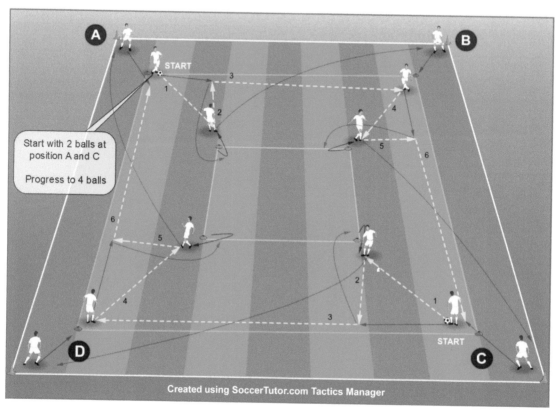

Start with 2 balls at position A and C

Progress to 4 balls

Created using SoccerTutor.com Tactics Manager

**Objective:** To improve passing, receiving and movements needed to provide support. Vicente Del Bosque has always been eager to work on keeping the ball, movement and creating space.

## Description

Mark out a 5 yard square inside a larger 15 yard square. Start with 2 balls in opposite corners (A & C). The practice is about keeping the ball moving using short and long passes, incorporating support play. The players check away each time to receive and move to the next positions after each pass.

**Progression:** Play with 4 balls and/or limit the players to 1 touch.

## Coaching Points

1. The timing of the pass and support is key, making sure the ball is played ahead of the next player to run onto and the supporting movement is timed well (not too early!).
2. The players and the ball should be constantly moving.
3. Encourage the players to receive half turned and with their head up to best see the next pass.

**Source:** Vicente Del Bosque's Real Madrid training drills from an interview conducted by Paco Cordobés and published by **abfutbol.es**

*Del Bosque, Emery, Benítez & Luis Enrique*

# 2. Passing Square: Short and Long Quick Combination Play

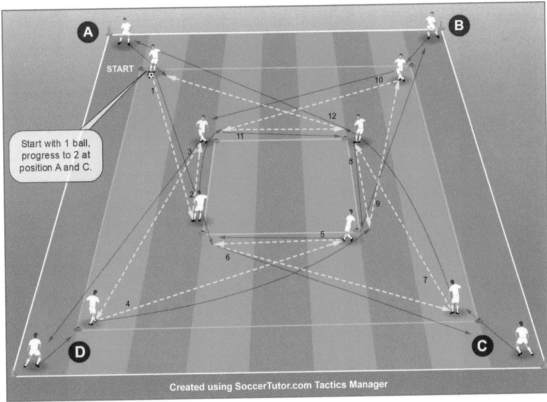

**Objective:** Short and long combination play with diagonal passing.

## Description

Using the same area as the previous practice, we now start with only 1 ball. We have 4 players starting on the inside and 4 on the outside. There are also 4 extra players (1 in each corner) waiting to go next.

The players play the passes as shown in the diagram, mixing short lay-off passes and long diagonal passes. The players check away each time to receive and move to the next positions after each pass.

**Progression:** Play with 2 balls from positions A and C.

## Coaching Points

1. The weight of the pass is key, making sure the ball is played ahead of the next player to run onto.
2. All passes need to be as accurate as possible to keep the ball moving quickly.

**Source:** Vicente Del Bosque's Real Madrid training drills from an interview conducted by Paco Cordobés and published by **abfutbol.es**

# VICENTE DEL BOSQUE

## Real Madrid Training Session 1

*Del Bosque, Emery, Benítez & Luis Enrique*

# 1. Fast Ball Circulation in a 9 v 9 (+2) Possession Game

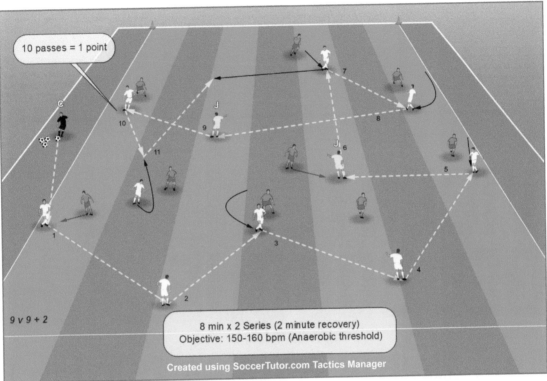

10 passes = 1 point

9 v 9 + 2

8 min x 2 Series (2 minute recovery)
Objective: 150-160 bpm (Anaerobic threshold)

Created using SoccerTutor.com Tactics Manager

**Objective:** Fast ball circulation and support play.

## Description

In a 40 x 50 yard area, we play a 9 v 9 (+2) possession game. The 2 yellow "jokers" play with the team in possession. All players are limited to 2 touches, but should use 1 touch when possible.

The team in possession (whites in diagram) try to complete 10 passes to score 1 point. The red defending team try to win the ball, and then they have the same aim.

**Conditioning:** Play 2 sets of 8 minutes with a 2 minute rest in between. The aim is to reach a heart rate of 150-160 bpm (high-intensity to reach anaerobic threshold).

## Coaching Points

1. Spread out and provide good width/depth to maintain possession.
2. Form effective triangles to offer support angles, open up to receive and keep the ball moving.
3. Play quick, precise, driven passes along the ground and signal where you want the ball delivered.

---

**Source:** Vicente Del Bosque's Real Madrid training sessions from an interview conducted by Paco Cordobés and published by **abfutbol.es**

*Del Bosque, Emery, Benítez & Luis Enrique*

# 2. 6 (+2) v 6 (+2) Possession Game with Rotating Outside Players

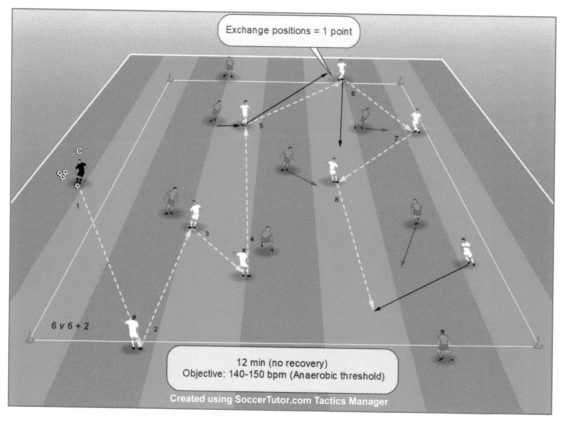

## Description

In a 40 x 50 yard area, each team has 6 players inside and 2 players outside at either end. All players are limited to 2 touches, but should use 1 touch when possible.

The coach starts by passing to one team and the aim is to maintain possession and pass to an outside player. When this happens, the outside player enters the area and the player who passed the ball moves outside (exchange positions). If this is achieved without losing the ball, 1 point is scored.

The defending team try to win the ball and then they continue with the same aims and rules.

**Conditioning:** Play 12 minutes without rest. The aim is to reach a heart rate of 140-150 bpm (high-intensity to reach anaerobic threshold).

**Coaching Point:** After a pass to an outside player, create good support angles to receive.

**Source:** Vicente Del Bosque's Real Madrid training sessions from an interview conducted by Paco Cordobés and published by **abfutbol.es**

# 3. Playing Forward Quickly in a 3 Zone 7 v 7 Small Sided Game

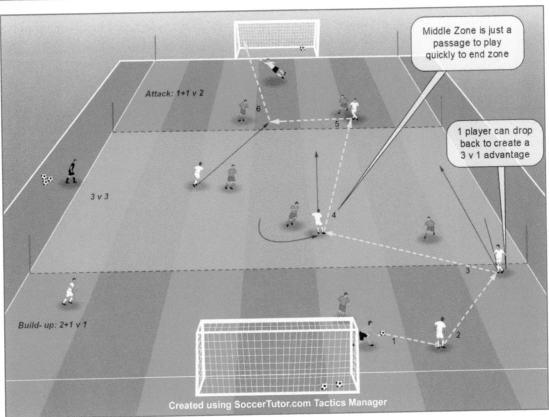

## Description

We start with 2 v 1 in the low zone, 3 v 3 in the middle zone and 1 v 2 in the high zone. When building up play, 1 player from the middle zone can drop back into the low zone, as shown in the diagram.

The ball is moved into the middle zone, which is just a passage to play the ball quickly into the high zone. Once the player receives in the high zone, 1 player can move forward from the middle zone to finish the attack (2 v 2). When the ball goes out or a goal is scored, start again with the other team.

The players are limited to 2 touches in the low/high zones and 1 touch in the middle zone.

**Conditioning:** Play 12 minutes without rest. The aim is to reach a heart rate of 150-160 bpm (high-intensity to reach anaerobic threshold).

**Coaching Point:** The key is to have the correct open body shape to receive and play a well-weighted driven pass along the ground into the high zone (using 1 touch).

**Source:** Vicente Del Bosque's Real Madrid training sessions from an interview conducted by Paco Cordobés and published by **abfutbol.es**

24

# VICENTE DEL BOSQUE

## Real Madrid Training Session 2

*Del Bosque, Emery, Benítez & Luis Enrique*

# 1. Dynamic 3 Team (6 + 6 v 6) Possession Game

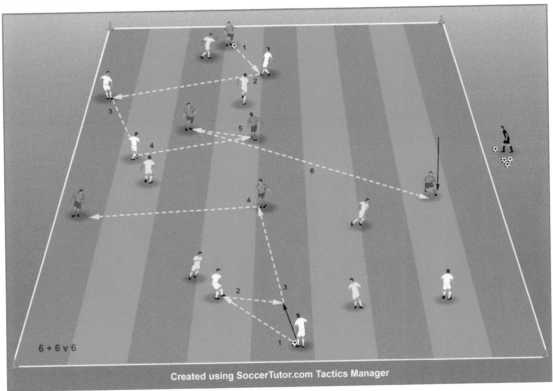

6 + 6 v 6

Created using SoccerTutor.com Tactics Manager

## Description

We have 3 teams and play with 2 balls simultaneously. 2 teams (whites and reds in diagram) maintain possession of both balls, utilising their numerical advantage (12 v 6) and the full size of the area.

The defending team (whites) try to win the ball. If they do, the team that lost the ball becomes the defending team and the practice continues.

**Conditioning:** Play 12 minutes without rest.

## Coaching Points

1.  Spread out and provide good width/depth to maintain possession. Form effective triangles to offer support angles, open up to receive and keep the ball moving.

2.  Play quick, driven passes along the ground and signal where you want the ball.

3.  Emphasise playing 1 touch passes. If it's not possible, use good technique to receive and then pass with good awareness of supporting teammates.

**Source:** Vicente Del Bosque's Real Madrid training sessions from an interview conducted by Paco Cordobés and published by **abfutbol.es**

*Del Bosque, Emery, Benítez & Luis Enrique*

# 2. Coordination, Speed and Agility Circuits with Passing and Finishing

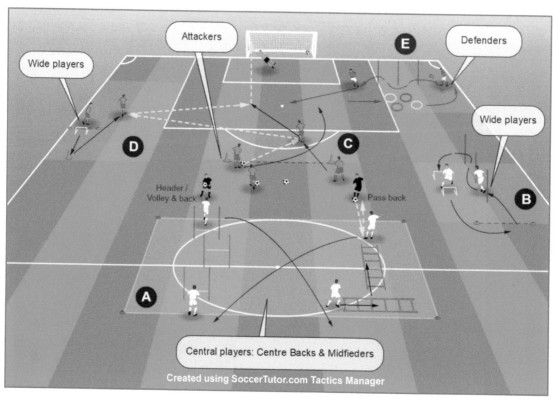

## Description

We split the players into 5 different stations (A. B, C, D & E) specific to their positions.

Stations A and B work within their areas continuously, but with adequate rest after each set. The players in Station B can swap with Station D halfway through the practice.

Stations C, D & E must work at the same time, so they can make sure they combine for the 2 v 1 attack shown in the diagram.

**A.** Sprint & Jump over 3 hurdles + header or volley / Quick steps through ladder + pass.

**B.** Slalom through poles, jump over 2 hurdles & sprint to start.

**C.** 1st player passes to 2nd player, who passes to D, runs into box & finishes.

**D.** Jump over hurdle, check back, run forward to receive and  pass into box for C's run.

**E.** Hop through the hoops, slalom through the poles and defend the goal.

---

**Source:** Vicente Del Bosque's Real Madrid training sessions from an interview conducted by Paco Cordobés and published by **abfutbol.es**

# 3. Playing Forward Quickly and Finishing in a 2 Zone Limited Area Game

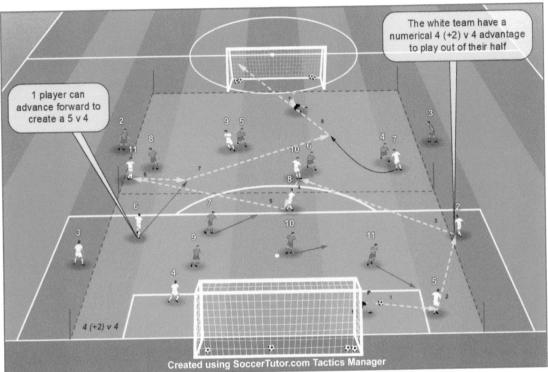

The white team have a numerical 4 (+2) v 4 advantage to play out of their half

1 player can advance forward to create a 5 v 4

4 (+2) v 4

Created using SoccerTutor.com Tactics Manager

## Description

We divide the area shown into 2 halves and play 11 v 11. Within each half, there is a 4 v 4 situation and both teams also have 2 players (full backs) as extra wide players outside.

The practice starts with the goalkeeper and the white team build up play. They use their numerical advantage to move the ball to one of their wide players (white No.2 in diagram). He then plays the ball into the attacking half.

From this point, 1 white player (No.6 in diagram) can move forward and the white team try to finish the attack as quickly as possible with a 5 v 4 situation.

When the ball goes out or a goal is scored, start again with the other team.

**Conditioning:** Play 20 minutes without rest. Finish the training session with 4 minutes stretching.

## Coaching Points

1. Move the ball forward from your half to the attacking half as quickly as possible.
2. Players in the attacking half need to check away from markers and create passing lines to receive.

**Source:** Vicente Del Bosque's Real Madrid training sessions from an interview conducted by Paco Cordobés and published by **abfutbol.es**

*Del Bosque, Emery, Benítez & Luis Enrique*

# VICENTE DEL BOSQUE

## Real Madrid Training Session 3

*Del Bosque, Emery, Benítez & Luis Enrique*

# 1. Dynamic Game with 2 Opposite Facing Goals in the Middle

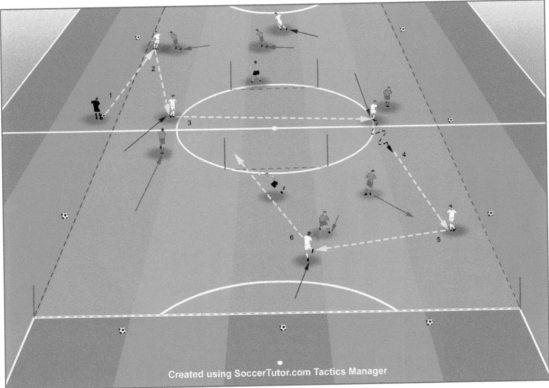

Created using SoccerTutor.com Tactics Manager

## Description

Mark out the area between the 2 penalty boxes and play a game with 2 teams of 6. There are also 2 goalkeepers defending goals facing in opposite directions, either side of the centre circle.

The practice starts with the goalkeeper and the team in possession (whites) try to use the full area to create space and score in either goal.

The defending team (reds) try to win the ball and then score themselves.

**Conditioning:** Play 20 minutes with 2 minutes' rest halfway through.

## Coaching Points

1. Encourage the attacking players to shoot when they create a yard of space.
2. The defending team needs to work together to apply pressing, to block the path to the goals and mark the potential receivers of the next pass.

**Source:** Vicente Del Bosque's Real Madrid training sessions from an interview conducted by Paco Cordobés and published by **abfutbol.es**

*Del Bosque, Emery, Benítez & Luis Enrique*

# 2. 1 v 1 / 2 v 2 Duels and 3 v 3 Game

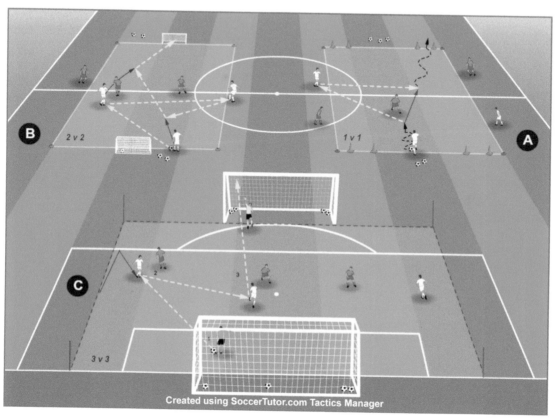

Created using SoccerTutor.com Tactics Manager

## Description

This practice splits the players into 3 groups:

**A.** 1 v 1 game with 2 small cone goals at either end. Points are scored by dribbling through the cones. The players can use their 2 outside players (who are limited to 1 touch) to get past their opponent.

**B.** 2 v 2 game with mini goals at either end. The players can use their outside player (who is limited to 1 touch) to get past their opponents.

**C.** Normal 3 v 3 game with 2 large goals and goalkeepers.

\* Finish the practice with 4 minutes of stretching.

**Source:** Vicente Del Bosque's Real Madrid training sessions from an interview conducted by Paco Cordobés and published by **abfutbol.es**

# 3. Playing Forward Quickly in a 3 Zone Game with Limited Touches (Del Bosque's Favourite Practice)

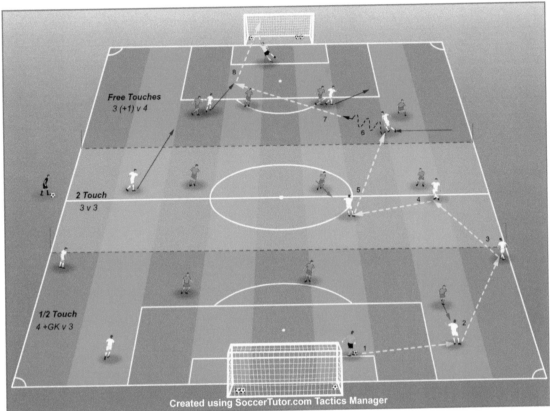

Created using SoccerTutor.com Tactics Manager

**Objective:** Vicente Del Bosque wants to move the ball forward and make the game fast. With this practice and the limited touches, players develop automatism to "play forward quickly."

## Description

We start with 4 (+GK) v 3 in the low zone, 3 v 3 in the middle zone and 3 v 4 in the high zone.

The white team start and they have a 5 v 3 advantage (with GK) to move the ball into the middle zone quickly. They then have a 3 v 3 situation in the middle zone and must move the ball to the final zone for a 3 +1 v 4 attack (1 white player from the middle zone moves forward to join the attack).

When the ball goes out or a goal is scored, start again with the other team.

## Coaching Points

1. Encourage creativity and push the players to enhance the different attacking possibilities.
2. Open body shape to receive and play a "well-weighted" accurate forward pass along the ground.

**Source:** Vicente Del Bosque's Real Madrid training sessions from an interview conducted by Paco Cordobés and published by **abfutbol.es**

# VICENTE DEL BOSQUE

## Real Madrid Training Session 4

*Del Bosque, Emery, Benítez & Luis Enrique*

# 1. Passing "Y" Shape: One-Two + Receive and Shoot

Created using SoccerTutor.com Tactics Manager

## Description

The players check away from the mannequins (marker) before receiving each pass. With the players positioned in a "Y" shape, Player A plays a 1-2 combination with B and then passes first time to C. Player C checks outside, then moves inside to receive and shoot.

The players all rotate positions (A -> B -> C -> Start) and the sequence is repeated on the left side.

**Conditioning:** Play for 20 minutes with 6-8 players (1-2 minutes' rest halfway through).

## Coaching Points

1. Passes need to be well-weighted and aimed in front of teammates, so they can run onto the ball.
2. The whole practice should be done at a high tempo.
3. The passes should all be done with 1 touch.
4. Player C needs to receive on the move and the first touch needs to be well judged and pushed out in front of the body and towards goal, ready to shoot.

**Source:** Vicente Del Bosque's Real Madrid training sessions from an interview conducted by Paco Cordobés and published by **abfutbol.es**

*Del Bosque, Emery, Benítez & Luis Enrique*

# 2. Passing "Y" Shape: Attacking Combination with Support Play

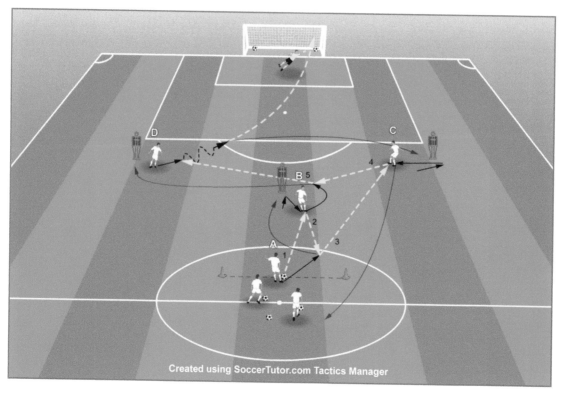

Created using SoccerTutor.com Tactics Manager

## Description

This is a variation of the previous practice. After A's pass to C, B turns and moves forward to receive a lay-off from C. Player B passes to D, who moves inside to receive and shoot at goal.

The players all rotate positions (A -> B -> C -> D -> Start) and the sequence is repeated on the other side, with Player C shooting at goal.

**Conditioning:** Play for 20 minutes with 6-8 players (1-2 minutes' rest halfway through).

## Coaching Points

1. When receiving with 1 foot and passing with the other, the first touch needs to be well judged and pushed out in front of the body.

2. Reduce the time between the first touch and the pass, and then progress to 1 touch when possible.

**Source:** Vicente Del Bosque's Real Madrid training sessions from an interview conducted by Paco Cordobés and published by **abfutbol.es**

_Del Bosque, Emery, Benítez & Luis Enrique_

# 3. Playing Out from the Back: Midfield Combinations or Direct Forward Pass

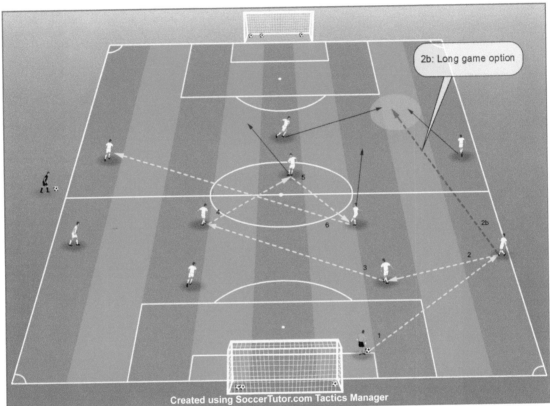

2b: Long game option

Created using SoccerTutor.com Tactics Manager

## Description

Football is a balance between the short and long game, depending on different tactical situations. In this practice, we work with the players on patterns of play to work the ball from the back to the front.

The pattern shown with the yellow arrows is one of Del Bosque's patterns of play for this situation. The players can practice a series of specific patterns determined by the coach during this 20 minute practice. However, you can also allow the defenders in possession to take a more direct route by playing directly to the forward players e.g. The right back's forward pass (2b) shown in the diagram.

The patterns that you practice and how you decide to work the ball from back to front can be varied in connection with changing game situations and the upcoming opponent's characteristics.

## Progressions

1. Allow the players to create their own patterns.
2. Add passive defenders, and then add active defenders.

**Source:** Vicente Del Bosque's Real Madrid training sessions from an interview conducted by Paco Cordobés and published by **abfutbol.es**

*Del Bosque, Emery, Benítez & Luis Enrique*

# 4. Playing Through the Centre and Fast Attacks in a Dynamic Game

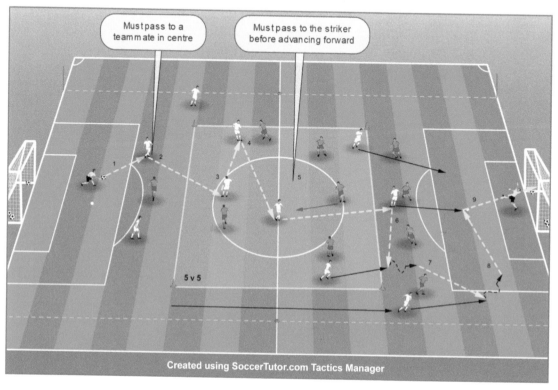

Must pass to a teammate in centre

Must pass to the striker before advancing forward

5 v 5

Created using SoccerTutor.com Tactics Manager

## Description

Both teams are in the 4-3-3 formation. You can adapt this to your formation. Inside the central area, both teams have 3 central midfielders and 2 wingers (5 v 5) and outside the central area, both teams have a goalkeeper, their back 4 and 1 forward.

The practice starts with the goalkeeper and one of the white defenders passes into the central area. The aim for the whites within this 5 v 5 area is to maintain possession and pass to the forward. If the reds win the ball within the central area, they launch a fast break attack to try and score.

As soon as the forward receives, the 2 wingers can leave the central area to support the forward and try to score a goal. You can also encourage the full backs to make overlapping runs, as shown in the diagram example. The 4 red defenders defend their goal. If a goal is scored or the ball goes out of play, restart with the red team's goalkeeper.

## Coaching Points

1. The forward must be constantly moving and create a passing line to receive.
2. The wingers must make direct forward runs to support the forward quickly.

---

**Source:** Vicente Del Bosque's Real Madrid training sessions from an interview conducted by Paco Cordobés and published by **abfutbol.es**

# UNAI EMERY

**This section includes:**

- Unai Emery Interview
- Unai Emery's Arsenal: A Tactical Analysis
- 16 Practices: Possession Games, Attacking Combination Play Practices, Finishing Practices and Small Sided Games (Arsenal & PSG)

# UNAI EMERY

*"I tell the players, the moment we stop working hard on this, as soon as we stop dedicating hours to this, we will fall."*

## Coaching Roles

- **Arsenal**
  (2018 - Present)
- **Paris Saint-Germain**
  (2016- 2018)
- **Sevilla**
  (2013 - 2016)
- **Valencia**
  (2008 - 2012)
- **Almería**
  (2006 - 2008)

## Honours

- **UEFA Europa League**
  (2014, 2015, 2016)
- **Ligue 1**
  (2018)
- **Coupe de France**
  (2017, 2018)
- **Coupe de la Ligue**
  (2017, 2018)
- **European Coach of the Season - European Union of Sports Press** (2014)

## Most Used Formations

- **4-3-3, 4-2-3-1, 3-4-3**

## Style of Play

"We are prepared to work with different systems. The 4-3-3 or 4-2-3-1 is the main system we use, it is great for keeping possession and applying pressure. But after that we need to have another system for different matches. Most importantly, it's getting the balance and positioning on the pitch with and without the ball."

"If you play every time, long balls, you lose possession and you lose momentum. I don't want to be like that."

## Coaching Philosophy

"My first target is not to win: it's to develop players with our work. That was my first idea when I started as a coach, because with this work comes results."

"The ball is a constant and we always try to have a section with the ball."

"We need to push. We need to have ambition. We need to have desire to improve every day."

## What it takes to be a Successful Coach

"What has led me to improve my preparation is taking my education while playing and learning everything, always being receptive to new knowledge."

"It is necessary to dedicate a lot of time and to have a group of players that are convinced of your methods."

"In football I work in the very short-term. I do not know who I'm playing against in two weeks. I'm not interested, I only live for the next game."

# UNAI EMERY

# Interview with Unai Emery

# INTERVIEW WITH UNAI EMERY

**SOURCE:** Unai Emery interview conducted by Juan Martín and published by **abfutbol.es**

**Is there any secret to explain your brilliant career?**

**Unai Emery:** "Possibly there is something that has marked me a lot, which is the taste I have for knowing the varieties that exist in football. Being a footballer, I was already thinking as a coach. That thought that I have had as a coach for a long time, is what has led me to improve my preparation, taking my degrees while playing and learning everything, always being receptive to new knowledge. All this, together with the experience of having been a professional player, has led me to have a more global vision, to be able to feel how a footballer suffers and enjoys."

**You play a brand of football which is both attractive and productive. What are the fundamental pillars on which this work is based?**

**UE:** "The objective is to win, it is to grow, it is to learn, but not only me as a coach, nor my assistants, but everyone, from the city, to the club president. You will learn and you will improve and the most important thing is to adapt quickly to new demands. Know your rivals, quickly know your team, to get the most out of it, know which system is the best, how you can act better with your players and all that is given to you by the day, living it with perseverance, with intensity and above all, looking for information and knowledge."

**The transitions in football are a key aspect that determine the quality and collective work of a team. How does that change of attack to defence or defence to attack mentality work?**

**UE:** "The training is what will take you to the match at the weekend, and in the end the training has to be as close to real match situations as possible. Of all these situations, one of the most important are the transitions, being quick to attack and quick to defend and that is where we finally know our best attributes and the weaknesses of the opponents, so that starting from that situation, we look for the better option, faster or slower, counter-attack or organised attack, always with a final goal, which is the maximum performance of your model."

**A team always starts from a good attacking organisation to overcome their opponent, but people talk a lot about "duels." What do you think about it? Is it such a determining factor?**

**UE:** "It is clear that football is one versus eleven, but all over the pitch there are individual duels. These duels can be improved and you can look for efficiency, matching the individual duels with the characteristics of a specific opponent or player. But what I think is more important, is to promote those individual duels, in which the player has the maximum knowledge of their rival, of his strengths, and has the maximum confidence to carry them out. There is another important factor in these individual duels, which is the mental aspect, the ability of one to concentrate on anticipating, be faster (mentally), and all this is trainable. It is a basic capacity that you have to achieve in the team, individually and in groups."

**What is never missing from your training?**

**UE:** "The ball is a constant and we always try to have a section with the ball. I think that for a footballer, the joy of carrying the work with maximum responsibility is given by the ball."

**Source:** Unai Emery interview conducted by Juan Martín and published by **abfutbol.es**

## How do you get your ideas to reach all the players?

UE: "We sequence them, first in the visual aspect with video or with explanations on a blackboard, and then in the theoretical aspect, taking on the pitch and analytically training all the aspects that you want from your team, both in defence and attack. Afterwards, this work is analysed with video and we can see if it is achieved or not, before then trying to reinforce it."

## How important is variation?

UE: "One of the main objectives I have is not to be monotonous, not to be very repetitive because it tires the players. There are things that you cannot vary but many other things you can. I try to make every training session I do different. Although we need variation, we also need a formed structure for the training week in terms of recovery, to prevent tiredness and injury. On Monday we train after the game (recovery session), on Tuesday we rest to recover and Wednesday and Thursday you can do two strong sessions to get the most out of your players. I am also in favour of resting on Monday to start training on Tuesday. In this way, Tuesday begins the training, Wednesday and Thursday have a high workload to prepare the game, and on Friday and Saturday we lower that load, but this is when we have to emphasise the knowledge and the tactical plan more, the way in which we want to play the game on Sunday."

## Do you use technology to improve player performance and prepare your team?

UE: "It is essential to advance, improve, progress. I always say to the players: "I would feel satisfied if with me the coach and my assistants, you learn something," and I should be a coach that is a better coach tomorrow than today. And for this, it is essential to use new technology. Logically, there are many things and you have to choose. You cannot work with all of them, but I think it is very important to advance in that. We try to

do it, we go gradually, we work with programs to dissect our performances and those of our opponents. We incorporate new technologies into the training. However, it creates more work, so you have to know what can be achieved and delegate to people who are capable to do it."

## How do you prepare a game and what do you emphasise most?

UE: "In football I work in the very short-term. I do not know who I'm playing against in two weeks. I'm not interested, I only live for the next game. How do I prepare? After the end of the game on Sunday, I am looking for all the information for the next opponent, especially with Juan Carlos Carcedo (assistant). Between the two of us, we look for all the possible information. On Monday and on Tuesday we start to prepare what we have to look at for in particular. Logically, we must bear in mind that the most important thing is us, what we are going to do. 70% of the focus is on analysing and improving everything to do with our team, and 30% about our opponent. We start preparing it on Monday and Tuesday and from there we look at the opponent and their characteristics. And at the end of the week, on Fridays and Saturdays, we start to give that information to the players, with the corresponding analysis to reinforce specific game situations. We focus on positive situations for the match, to build confidence in doing things, and that's a little bit of opponent preparation. Then, the training is based on that."

## What does a coach need to reach elite level?

UE: "It is necessary to dedicate a lot of time and to have a group of players that are convinced of your methods. Apart from work, you need to have good players. I like to say that "The better you do things, the more options you have to get it right," and maybe that's why I may be doing well, as we try to apply all our work and above all, have a human group that are good footballers."

Source: Unai Emery interview conducted by Juan Martín and published by abfutbol.es

*Del Bosque, Emery, Benítez & Luis Enrique*

# UNAI EMERY

## Arsenal: A Tactical Analysis

# Unai Emery's Formation and Tactics

## Unai Emery's Arsenal Formations (4-2-3-1, 3-4-3 & 3-4-1-2)

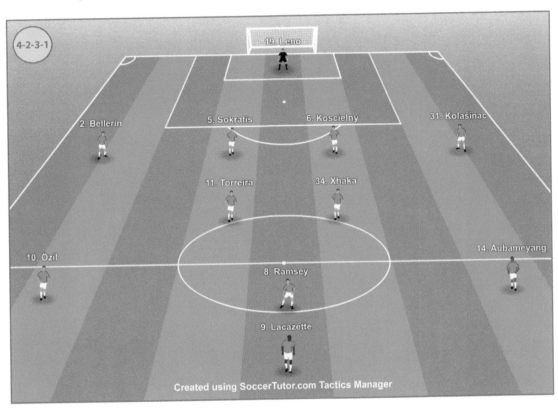

Unai Emery's teams are hard-working with aggressive pressing tactics and he likes to adjust his strategy based on the opponent. This is the main reason why he uses different formations throughout the season.

Emery's basic 4-2-3-1 formation at Arsenal is based on the characteristics of his players (see diagram above). This formation was used half of the time and is the focus of our tactical analysis.

The variations we have seen most notably throughout the 2018-2019 season are the 3-4-3 (or 3-4-2-1) and the 3-4-1-2 formation.

These 2 variations are displayed on the following page with examples of when Emery used them successfully against strong opposition in the Premier League (Tottenham and Manchester United).

**Source:** Unai Emery's Arsenal tactical analysis by **Tsaniklidis Giannis**, Match Analyst at PAOK FC U17 (Greece)

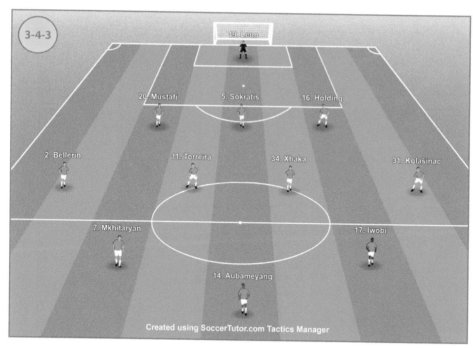

* Also referred to as 3-4-2-1

Emery used the 3-4-3 formation in the 4-2 Premier League win against Tottenham on 2nd December 2018, utilising the width against Spurs' 4-1-2-1-2 formation.

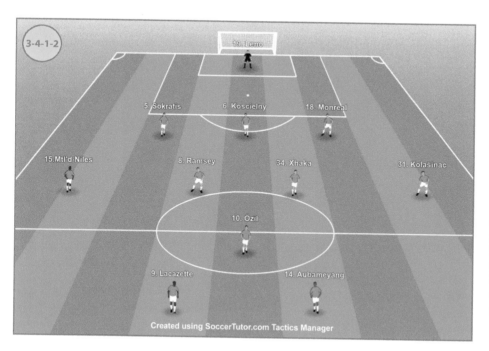

Emery used the 3-4-1-2 formation in the 2-0 Premier League win against Manchester United on 10th March 2019, utilising more attacking players than usual to overload United's vulnerable defence.

**Source:** Unai Emery's Arsenal tactical analysis by **Tsaniklidis Giannis**, Match Analyst at PAOK FC U17 (Greece)

# Unai Emery's Tactics in the Build-Up Phase

In the build-up and attacking phase, Emery's Arsenal have shown a flexibility in their combination play and their movement, but there are some fixed patterns of play that we analyse in this section.

## 1. Building Up Play from the Back with a Switch Along the Back Line (4-2-3-1)

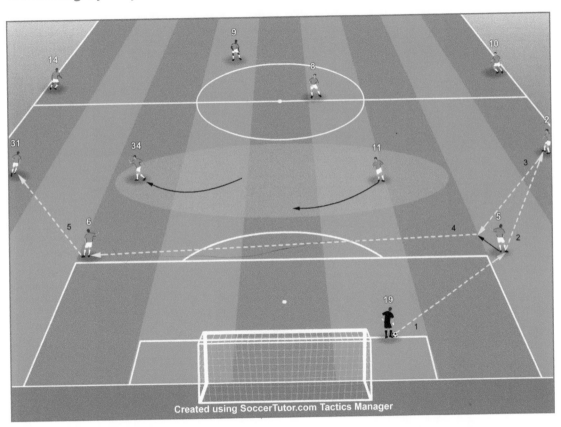

Created using SoccerTutor.com Tactics Manager

As a technical team that likes to keep possession of the ball, Emery's Arsenal build up attacks from the defensive third.

In the first phase, we see a flank-to-flank ball transfer with small passes between the GK and the defensive line. The full backs **Bellerín (2)** and **Kolašinac (31)** are positioned high.

The defensive midfielders **Xhaka (34)** and **Torreira (11)** drop low and towards the strong side to create passing options for their defenders.

The left back **Kolašinac (31)** receives out wide and looks to progress the attack.

**Source:** Unai Emery's Arsenal tactical analysis by **Tsaniklidis Giannis**, Match Analyst at PAOK FC U17 (Greece)

*Del Bosque, Emery, Benítez & Luis Enrique*

## 2. Winger on the Strong Side Drops Back to Provide a Passing Option (4-2-3-1)

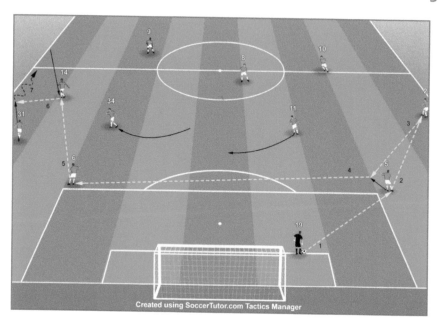

In this variation to the previous example, **Koscielny (6)** doesn't pass to **Kolašinac (31)**. **Xhaka (34)** and **Torreira (11)** have moved across to create a strong side. The left winger **Aubameyang (14)** drops back to create a passing option for **Koscielny (6)**.

**Aubameyang (14)** is used as a link player to play the ball to **Kolašinac (31)**, who dribbles forward.

## 3. Passing Options for the Deep Central Midfielder (4-2-3-1)

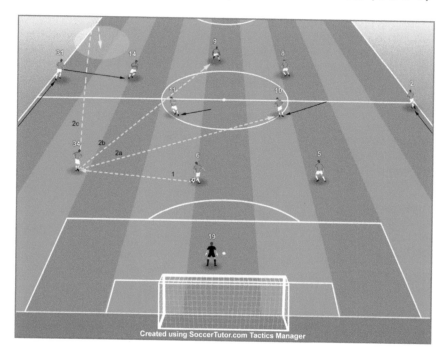

In this variation of the previous diagram, **Koscielny (6)** passes to central midfielder **Xhaka (34)**, who has moved across. His first passing option (2a) is to the playmaker **Özil (10)**, who is behind the pressure zone.

**Koscielny (6)** can also pass forward to striker **Lacazette (9)** or out wide for the forward run of **Kolašinac (31)**. **Aubameyang (14)** has moved inside to create space.

---

**Source:** Unai Emery's Arsenal tactical analysis by **Tsaniklidis Giannis**, Match Analyst at PAOK FC U17 (Greece)

*Del Bosque, Emery, Benítez & Luis Enrique*

## 4. Exploiting Space in Behind the Opposition's High Defensive Line (4-2-3-1)

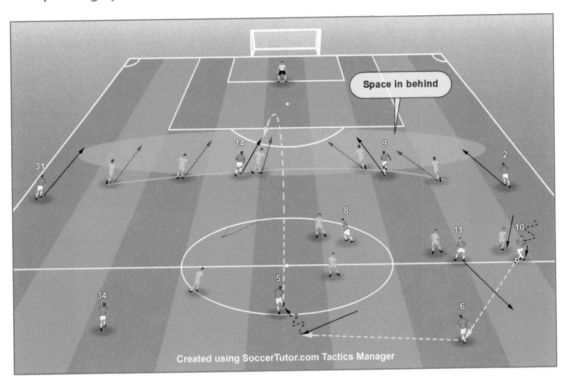

Created using SoccerTutor.com Tactics Manager

This tactical example shows how Unai Emery's Arsenal sometimes vary their game and use direct passes to utilise their fast forwards.

Arsenal look to exploit the space available in behind when the opposition have a high defensive line.

In this example, the centre back **Sokratis (5)** is free in space, the opposition are unable to prevent him from playing forward and there is available space in behind their defence.

**Sokratis (5)** plays a direct pass over the top of the opposition's defence for the left winger **Aubameyang (14)** to run onto, with support from the striker **Lacazette (9)**.

**Aubameyang (14)** receives in behind and Arsenal have a good chance to score a goal.

This tactic is used by Emery's Arsenal when the defender in possession has little to no pressure on the ball and there is space available in behind the opposition's defensive line.

The aggressive speed of **Aubameyang** and **Lacazette** is the key to the success of this tactic.

**Source:** Unai Emery's Arsenal tactical analysis by **Tsaniklidis Giannis**, Match Analyst at PAOK FC U17 (Greece)

*Del Bosque, Emery, Benítez & Luis Enrique*

# Unai Emery's Tactics in the Creating Phase

After Unai Emery's Arsenal team safely move the ball to the next zone (middle third), they then use the following tactics to create space and move into the final stage of attack:

**A.** Overloading of the central areas, with the width being created by the full backs.

**B.** Mobility to create space and passing options, as well as a numerical advantage where needed.

**C.** Switching of positions - one player moves forward and another drops back into the space (in sync).

**D.** Positioning players between the lines (mainly **Ramsey**, **Özil** or **Lacazette**).

## 1. Ball Circulation to Move the Ball Out Wide to the Full Back (4-2-3-1)

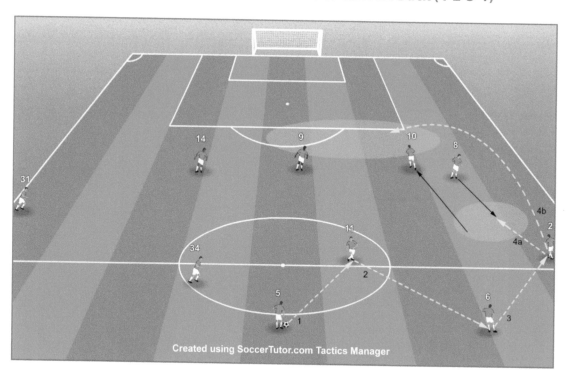

Created using SoccerTutor.com Tactics Manager

Arsenal combine to move the ball out wide to right back **Bellerín (2)**, who is free in space. As the ball is travelling to **Bellerín (2)**, the right winger **Mesut Özil (10)** makes a forward run. At the same time, the attacking midfielder **Aaron Ramsey (8)** drops back into the space created.

**Bellerín (2)** can now either pass to **Ramsey (8)** in the space created or play a through ball in behind the opposition's defensive line for **Özil's (10)** well-timed forward run - please see the following page to see how the attack develops.

---

**Source:** Unai Emery's Arsenal tactical analysis by **Tsaniklidis Giannis**, Match Analyst at PAOK FC U17 (Greece)

---

*Del Bosque, Emery, Benítez & Luis Enrique*

## 2. Passing Options for the Full Back After Players Switch Positions (4-2-3-1)

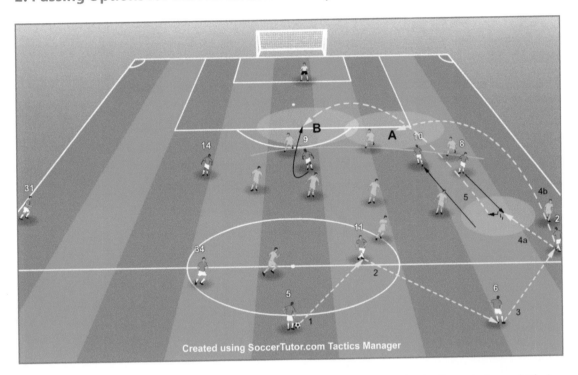

Created using SoccerTutor.com Tactics Manager

This is a continuation of the example on the previous page. The right back **Bellerín (2)** has possession of the ball.

The right winger **Mesut Özil (10)** has made a run forward, which creates space for the attacking midfielder **Aaron Ramsey (8)** to drop back into.

The easiest and safest option is to play a short pass to **Ramsey (8)** and Arsenal will maintain possession of the ball.

However, due to this switching of positions from **Özil (10)** and **Ramsey (8)**, Arsenal have a potential 2 v 2 or 3 v 2 situation in the penalty area against the opposing centre back and right back.

**Özil (10)**, **Lacazette (9)** and **Aubameyang (14)** are all positioned between the lines and ready to make runs in behind.

Therefore, **Bellerín's (2)** second option is to play a pass in behind the opposition's defensive line, as shown (2 options: A and B).

This tactic is used a lot by Emery's Arsenal. Their attacking players are fast and adept at running onto through balls, often leading to goal scoring opportunities.

---

**Source:** Unai Emery's Arsenal tactical analysis by **Tsaniklidis Giannis**, Match Analyst at PAOK FC U17 (Greece)

*Del Bosque, Emery, Benítez & Luis Enrique*

# Unai Emery's Tactics in the Finishing Phase

After Unai Emery's Arsenal team move into the final third, they use the following tactics to create goal scoring opportunities:

**A.** Overload the central channel to allow the full backs to receive with plenty of space to cross.

**B.** Fast synchronised movement from the attackers and midfielders.

**C.** Players attack the gaps to receive a pass in behind the defensive line.

**D.** Very fast combinations with 1 or 2 touches.

## 1. Passing Options for the Full Back After Players Switch Positions (4-2-3-1)

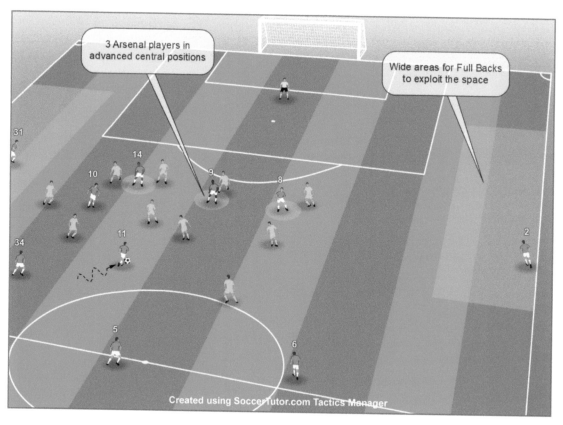

The opposition's entire back 4 are occupied by 3 Arsenal players (**8, 9 & 14**), which leaves the wide areas free for the full backs to exploit. The objective is to move the ball out wide for the full back to cross and have 3-5 players make runs into the box to try and score.

---

**Source:** Unai Emery's Arsenal tactical analysis by **Tsaniklidis Giannis**, Match Analyst at PAOK FC U17 (Greece)

## 2. Full Back Crossing from Wide with 5 Players Making Runs into Box (4-2-3-1)

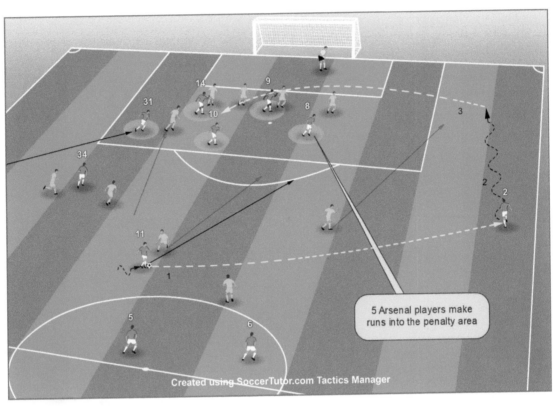

5 Arsenal players make runs into the penalty area

In this tactical example, Arsenal's right back **Bellerín (2)** receives out wide from **Torreira (11)** and dribbles forward.

The opposing left winger is not able to get out to him in time, so **Bellerín (2)** can cross freely into the penalty area.

Arsenal always look to have 3-5 players make runs into the penalty area in this situation, thus creating a good opportunity to score.

In this tactical example, 5 Arsenal players make runs into the penalty area:

1. Attacking midfielder **Ramsey (8)** runs to the near post.

2. Striker **Lacazette (9)** runs into a central area, approaching the 6-yard box.

3. Left winger **Aubameyang (14)** runs to the far post.

4. Right winger **Özil (10)** runs to the edge of the area, ready for a cut back, a clearance or a rebound.

5. Left back **Kolašinac (31)** arrives from the other side.

---

**Source:** Unai Emery's Arsenal tactical analysis by **Tsaniklidis Giannis**, Match Analyst at PAOK FC U17 (Greece)

*Del Bosque, Emery, Benítez & Luis Enrique*

## 3. Attacking the Gaps in the Defensive Line to Receive in Behind (4-2-3-1)

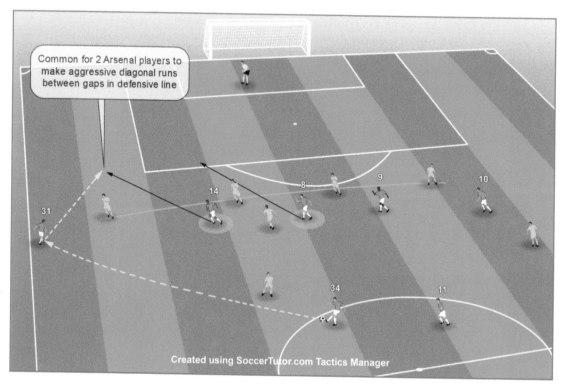

Common for 2 Arsenal players to make aggressive diagonal runs between gaps in defensive line

Created using SoccerTutor.com Tactics Manager

This is a variation of the previous tactical example. This time, the left back **Kolašinac (31)** receives in space out wide from **Xhaka (34)**.

Instead of dribbling up the line and delivering a cross, **Kolašinac (31)** also has the option of playing a through pass to exploit the space in behind the opposition's defensive line.

Arsenal again have 3 players in advanced central positions **(8, 9 & 14)**, positioned between the lines.

Left winger **Aubameyang (14)** and attacking midfielder **Aaron Ramsey (8)** both make forward runs either side of the right centre back.

The left back **Kolašinac (31)** has time and space to play a good pass in behind for either of their runs.

In this tactical example, **Kolašinac (31)** is able to successfully pass to **Aubameyang (14)**.

**Aubameyang (14)** is a very fast player and when he receives in behind, he can be very dangerous by dribbling quickly into the penalty area to either shoot at goal or provide a cross for an oncoming teammate.

**Source:** Unai Emery's Arsenal tactical analysis by **Tsaniklidis Giannis**, Match Analyst at PAOK FC U17 (Greece)

*Del Bosque, Emery, Benítez & Luis Enrique*

# UNAI EMERY

## Technical Practices

*"The mental aspect, the ability of one to concentrate on anticipating, be faster (mentally), all this is trainable."*

*Del Bosque, Emery, Benítez & Luis Enrique*

# 1. Four Colours - Quick Reactions, Vision and Awareness Practice

> 1    RED...
> 3    BLUE...
> 6    YELLOW...

Emery

Emery continues until the player receives a total of 4 balls

Created using SoccerTutor.com Tactics Manager

**Objective:** Awareness, vision, body shape + technical aspects of receiving and passing.

## Description

In a 10 yard square, there is 1 player in the centre and 4 feeder players with balls outside. Each mannequin goal (and outside feeder player) are assigned a different colour (red, blue, yellow, green).

The coach (Emery) calls out 3 colours in order:

1.  The coach calls out the first colour e.g. "RED."

2.  The player must move and touch the red mannequin.

3.  The coach calls out the second colour e.g. "BLUE."

4.  The player must move to receive a pass from that player (feeder by the blue goal).

5.  The blue feeder player passes to the central player.

6.  The coach calls out the third and final colour e.g. "YELLOW."

7.  The player must receive the pass with the correct body shape to quickly pass into the yellow goal.

**Source:** Unai Emery's PSG training session at Camp des Loges Training Ground, Paris - 10th January 2018

# 2. Open Up to Receive and Play Forward in a Passing Circuit

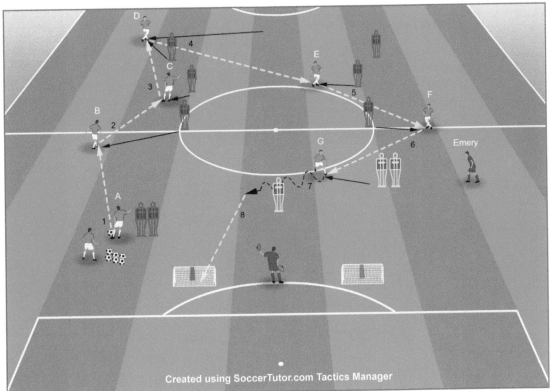

Created using SoccerTutor.com Tactics Manager

## Description

The practice starts from Player A and the players simply receive and pass forward to the next teammate (A -> B -> C -> D -> E -> F -> G) and then follow their pass.

The receiving players check away from their mannequin (defender), open up to receive on the half-turn and then pass forward.

Player D receives the pass on either side of the mannequin, but faces C who passed him the ball. He then changes the direction of play towards the goals with his pass to E. When G receives, he dribbles around the final mannequin and the coach lifts up a blue or red bib. Player G must be aware and then score in the right goal e.g. The blue goal in the diagram example.

**Coaching Point:** It appears as though Emery gives the players a free choice whether to receive the pass to the left or right of the mannequin - the passer must be aware of their teammate's movement.

**Source:** Unai Emery's Arsenal training session at Arsenal Training Centre, London Colney - 4th July 2018

*Del Bosque, Emery, Benítez & Luis Enrique*

# UNAI EMERY

## Possession Games

*Del Bosque, Emery, Benítez & Luis Enrique*

# 1. Positional End to End Possession Game with GKs

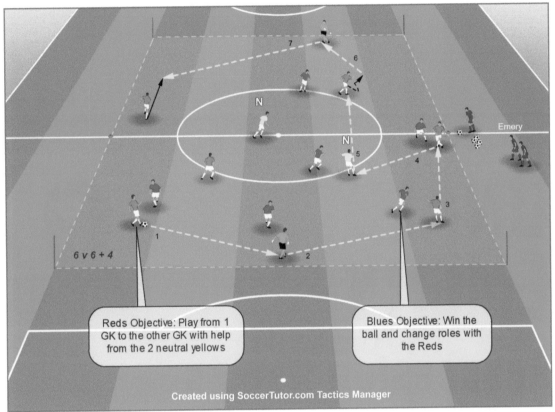

**Reds Objective:** Play from 1 GK to the other GK with help from the 2 neutral yellows

**Blues Objective:** Win the ball and change roles with the Reds

6 v 6 + 4

Emery

Created using SoccerTutor.com Tactics Manager

**Objective:** Positional and support play to maintain possession.

## Description

Within the area shown, we have 2 teams of 6 + 2 yellow neutral players and 2 neutral GKs.

The team in possession (reds in diagram) aim to move the ball from one GK to the other, with the help of the 2 yellow neutral players. If they achieve this, they continue the practice and try to move the ball back to the other GK.

The defending team (blues in diagram) work collectively to press and try to win the ball. If they are successful, they change roles with the reds and look to transfer the ball from one GK to the other.

**Source:** Unai Emery's Arsenal training session at Arsenal Training Centre, London Colney - 23rd November 2018

*Del Bosque, Emery, Benítez & Luis Enrique*

# 2. Possession and Switching the Point of Attack in a 4 Zone Game

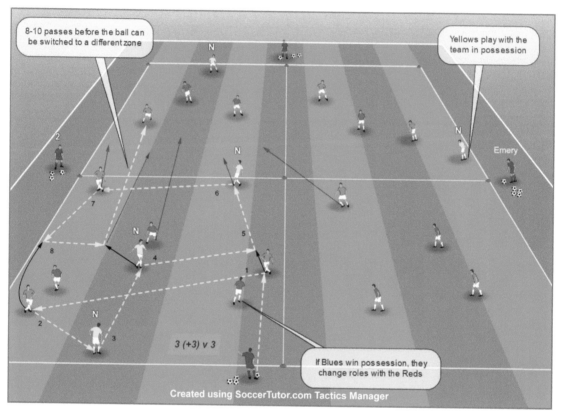

8-10 passes before the ball can be switched to a different zone

Yellows play with the team in possession

Emery

3 (+3) v 3

If Blues win possession, they change roles with the Reds

Created using SoccerTutor.com Tactics Manager

**Objective:** Positional and support play to maintain possession and switch the point of attack.

## Description

In a 20 x 20 yard area, we have 2 teams 8 players + 5 yellow neutral players who play with the team in possession.

The practice starts with the coach's pass into one of the zones, where there is a 3 v 3 (+3) situation. The red team aim to maintain possession within that square and complete 8-10 passes. The rest of the players are waiting (spread out) in the other 3 zones.

Once 8-10 passes are completed, the reds pass the ball to a teammate in another zone. The players need to be aware to recreate the same 3 v 3 (+3) situation with players moving into this zone. The practice continues with the same aim.

If the defending team (blues) win the ball at any time, they change roles with the red team.

---

**Source:** Unai Emery's Arsenal training session at Arsenal Training Centre, London Colney - 5th July 2018

*Del Bosque, Emery, Benítez & Luis Enrique*

# UNAI EMERY

## Warm-Up Circuits

# 1. Speed and Agility Warm-Up Circuit

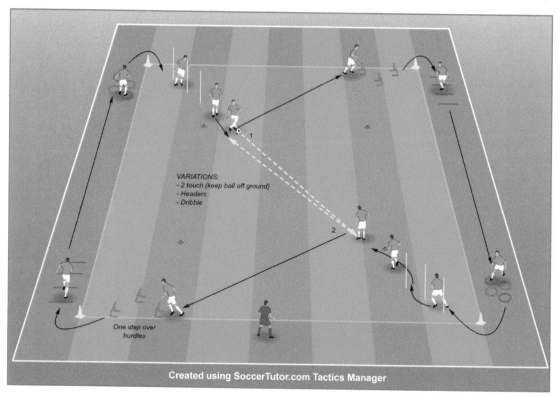

VARIATIONS:
- 2 touch (keep ball off ground)
- Headers
- Dribble

One step over hurdles

Created using SoccerTutor.com Tactics Manager

**Objective:** Warm-up with coordination, speed and agility training.

## Description

The players start in the centre and play 1 pass before moving to their left and starting the circuit.

Each corner of the circuit has different speed, coordination and agility components.

When each player reaches the corner with the poles, he slaloms through them and plays a pass before continuing around the circuit.

**Source:** Unai Emery's Arsenal training session at Arsenal Training Centre, London Colney - 31st August 2018

*Del Bosque, Emery, Benítez & Luis Enrique*

# 2. Accurate Finishing Warm-Up Circuit

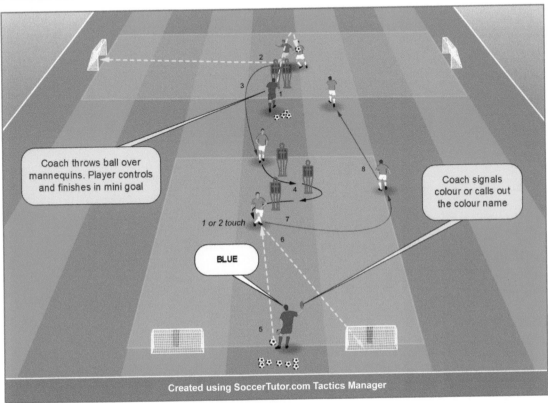

Coach throws ball over mannequins. Player controls and finishes in mini goal

Coach signals colour or calls out the colour name

1 or 2 touch

BLUE

Created using SoccerTutor.com Tactics Manager

**Objective:** Technical warm-up with awareness elements.

## Description

The players start in the different positions shown and move round in a circuit between the 2 different areas.

1. In the 1st area, the coach throws a ball over the 2 mannequins and the player must control the ball with 1 touch and then score in either mini goal with his 2nd touch. He then moves to the other area and the next player goes.

2. In the 2nd area, the players move using sidesteps through the mannequins. The coach signals a colour (visually or calls out) and the player must score in that mini goal. Variations include the player using 1 or 2 touches and the coach passing along the ground or throwing the ball up in the air for a header.

**Source:** Unai Emery's Arsenal training session at Arsenal Training Centre, London Colney - 5th July 2018

*Del Bosque, Emery, Benítez & Luis Enrique*

# UNAI EMERY

## Attacking Combination Play

# 1. Attacking Combination with Overlap, Cut-Back, Finish + Rebound

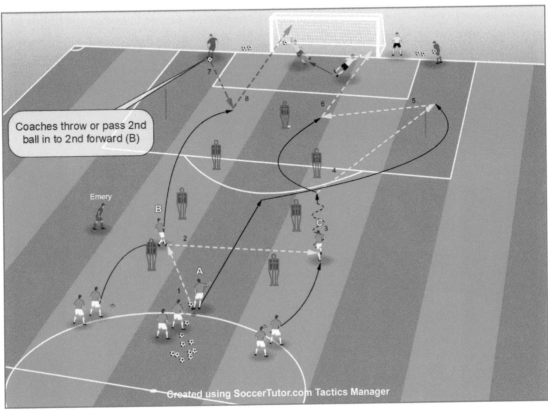

Coaches throw or pass 2nd ball in to 2nd forward (B)

**Objective:** Quick combination play, timing of movement, weight of pass and finishing.

## Description

The players work in groups of 3 with the following combination:

1. All 3 players start on the red cones. Player A passes to B, who moves around the mannequin to receive. Player A runs forward.

2. B passes across for C to run onto. B makes a run into the penalty area towards the far post.

3. C dribbles forward at the mannequin, while A makes an overlapping run.

4. C passes to A on the overlap, who has run around the pole.

5. A cuts the ball back for C.

6. C shoots and tries to score.

7. The coach throws or passes a 2nd ball to the other forward (B) to try and score.

**Source:** Unai Emery's Arsenal training session during preseason tour in Singapore - 24th July 2018

# 2. Attacking Combination with Overlap and Finish + Rebound

Coaches throw or pass 2nd ball in to 2nd forward (B) & apply pressure

**Objective:** Quick combination play, timing of movement, weight of pass and finishing.

## Description

The players work in groups of 3 with the following combination:

1. The 3 players start in a vertical line as shown. A passes to B who, moves off to his left to receive. Player A runs around to the right.

2. B dribbles forward.

3. B passes across to C who, has moved off his cone in front of the mannequin to receive.

4. C dribbles forward.

5. C passes to A on the overlap, who has run around the pole.

6. A shoots and tries to score.

7. The coach throws/passes a 2nd ball to the other forward (B) and applies pressure to his shot.

**Source:** Unai Emery's Arsenal training session during preseason tour in Singapore - 24th July 2018

*Del Bosque, Emery, Benítez & Luis Enrique*

# UNAI EMERY

## Finishing Practices

*"Duels can be improved and you can look for efficiency, matching the individual duels with the characteristics of a specific opponent or player. But what I think is more important, is to promote those individual duels, in which the player has the maximum knowledge of their rival, of his strengths, and has the maximum confidence to carry them out."*

# 1. One-Two, Dribble and Finish

**Objective:** Dribbling to beat a defender, create space to shoot and finish.

## Description

The coaches set up the mannequins in different ways to vary the situation for the players and these are changed constantly during the practice.

The players play a 1-2 with Emery and then dribble forward. They are confronted by a coach (passive defender) and they must dribble around him using 1 v 1 techniques.

The player then tries to score past the goalkeeper and the next player goes.

## Variation

The players vary their start position (central and left cones), as does the coach.

---

**Source:** Unai Emery's Arsenal training session at Arsenal Training Centre, London Colney - 23rd November 2018

*Del Bosque, Emery, Benítez & Luis Enrique*

# 2. Receive with Back to Goal, One-Two and Finish

Emery bounces the ball to player

Emery varies the service by passing from stationary and moving with the ball

Coach uses a "crash pad" to apply pressure to player

Created using SoccerTutor.com Tactics Manager

**Objective:** Receiving with back to goal, shielding the ball, quick one-touch play and turning.

## Description

The players are spread out in positions A to C.

Unai Emery bounces the ball to Player A, who has a coach behind him with a crash pad to apply pressure. Player A must receive with his back to goal, while shielding the ball and pass to Player B.

Player B passes ahead of A to run onto (1-2 combination) and A tries to score past the goalkeeper. We then continue the practice on the other side with Player C.

Emery varies the service throughout the practice by throwing from a stationary position and while moving with the ball.

**Variation:** The players simply receive, turn and shoot (no 1-2 combination).

**Source:** Unai Emery's Arsenal training session at Arsenal Training Centre, London Colney - 6th March 2019

*Del Bosque, Emery, Benítez & Luis Enrique*

# 3. One-Two to Receive in Behind and Finish + Rebound

> Ball is always served to the 2nd forward unless he attempts from a rebound

Created using SoccerTutor.com Tactics Manager

**Objective:** Quick combination play and finishing.

## Description

The players work in pairs with the following combination:

1. The coach passes to Player A.
2. Player A passes across to B.
3. Player B passes into the penalty area for A, who has run around the mannequin (1-2 combination).
4. Player A tries to score past the goalkeeper.
5. The coach throws or passes a 2nd ball to Player B (unless there was a rebound from A's shot).
6. Player B tries to score with a first time shot.

**Source:** Unai Emery's Arsenal training session at Arsenal Training Centre, London Colney - 13th July 2018

*Del Bosque, Emery, Benítez & Luis Enrique*

# 4. Timing Runs into the Penalty Area and Precise Finishing + Rebound

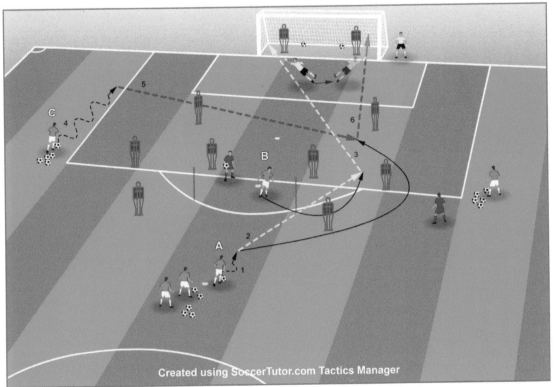

Created using SoccerTutor.com Tactics Manager

**Objective:** Opening up to receive and finish.

## Description

**1.** Player A dribbles forward and B runs around the pole.

**2.** Player A passes into the penalty area.

**3.** Player B opens up his body to receive and then tries to score past the goalkeeper.

**4.** Player C dribbles forward.

**5.** Player C crosses the 2nd ball into the penalty area.

**6.** Player A has run around the mannequins and tries to score from Player C's cross.

**7.** Repeat the practice on the opposite side.

---

**Source:** Unai Emery's Arsenal training session at Arsenal Training Centre, London Colney - 14th September 2018

*Del Bosque, Emery, Benítez & Luis Enrique*

# 5. One v One, Cross and Finish + Rebound

> If no rebound, a ball is thrown or passed to 2nd forward

**Objective:** Dribbling to beat a defender, crossing and finishing.

## Description

1. Player A passes to the yellow defender.

2. The yellow defender passes back (1-2 combination).

3. Player A passes out wide to B and the yellow defender moves to contest him.

4. Player B must get beyond the defender to create space for a cross.

5. Player B crosses the ball into the penalty area for C and D, who have made forward runs.

6. Either C or D can try to score (C in diagram) and the other player is alert to the rebound (D).

7. If there is no rebound from Player C's shot, then the coach throws a 2nd ball in for Player D to try and score with a 1 touch finish.

**Source:** Unai Emery's Arsenal training session at Arsenal Training Centre, London Colney - 12th July 2018

*Del Bosque, Emery, Benítez & Luis Enrique*

# UNAI EMERY

## Small Sided Games

# 1. Fast Attacks and Transitions in a 3 Team Game

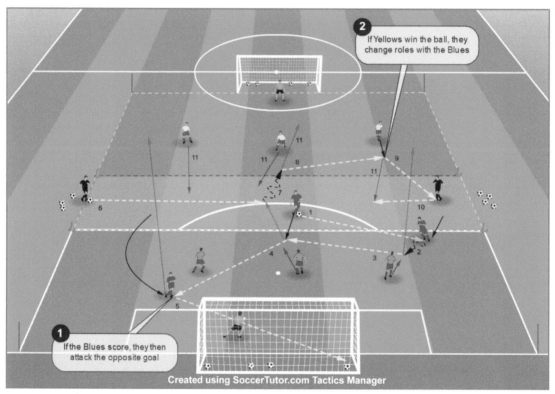

**2** If Yellows win the ball, they change roles with the Blues

**1** If the Blues score, they then attack the opposite goal

Created using SoccerTutor.com Tactics Manager

**Objective:** Fast combination play to score quickly + transitions.

## Description

The 3 teams start in 3 different zones and the practice starts with the navy team in the middle zone.

The navy team play forward and attack the red team with fast combination play, trying to score past the goalkeeper as quickly as possible.

If the navy team score, they then receive a new ball from the coach in the middle zone and attack the yellows. They continue to attack either end as long as they keep scoring. If they don't score, the reds will move to the middle zone and attack the yellows with a new ball.

If a defending team wins the ball (yellows in diagram example), they pass to the coach in the middle zone immediately and then attack the team at the other end (reds). In this situation, the navy team move to the yellow team's end, waiting to defend in the next phase.

---

**Source:** Unai Emery's PSG training session at Camp des Loges Training Ground, Paris - 10th January 2018

*Del Bosque, Emery, Benítez & Luis Enrique*

# 2. Small Sided Game with GK End Zones and 4 Mini Goals

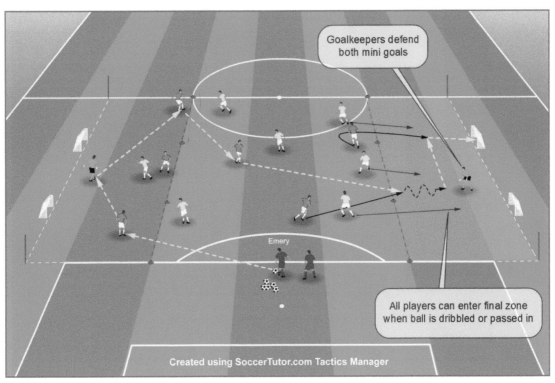

Goalkeepers defend both mini goals

All players can enter final zone when ball is dribbled or passed in

Emery

Created using SoccerTutor.com Tactics Manager

**Objective:** Build-up, ball circulation, attacking combination play and finishing.

## Description

In the area shown, Unai Emery plays a 7 v 7 small sided game with the end zones marked out. The GKs defend both mini goals at their end.

Emery starts the practice by passing to a red player in an end zone. For the moment, the 2 teams play within 2 zones and the reds aim to move the ball into the end zone.

The yellow team work together to try and win the ball. If they succeed, the team roles are reversed.

The reds either dribble or pass into the end zone and try to score. All players from both teams can enter the end zone once the ball is dribbled or passed in there.

If a goal is scored or the ball goes out of play, Emery passes in a new ball to the other team.

---

**Source:** Unai Emery's Arsenal training session at Arsenal Training Centre, London Colney - 5th July 2018

# 3. Finishing Game with Outside End Players

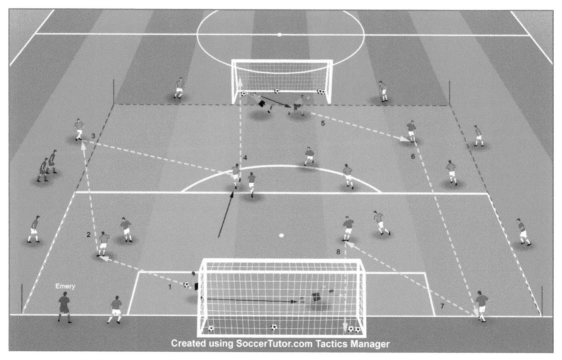

Created using SoccerTutor.com Tactics Manager

**Objective:** Creating space, shooting and finishing.

## Description

This is a normal game that starts from either goalkeeper. Each team has 5 players inside the area and 4 extra players outside in their attacking half.

The aim is to pass the ball to the outside players who play it back or cross the ball, ready for the inside players to shoot at goal.

This game encourages constant shooting and finishing practice, with lots of goals.

**Source:** Unai Emery's Arsenal training session at Arsenal Training Centre, London Colney - 17th August 2018

# RAFAEL BENÍTEZ

**This section includes:**

- **Rafael Benítez Interview**
- **2 Rafael Benítez Tactical Examples** (Liverpool)
- **2 Full Napoli Training Sessions** (10 Practices)

# RAFAEL BENÍTEZ

*"To win, you must be demanding and the players must understand that this requirement is for their benefit."*

## Coaching Roles

- **Newcastle United**
  (2016 - Present)
- **Real Madrid**
  (2015 - 2016)
- **Napoli**
  (2013–2015)
- **Chelsea (interim)**
  (2012–2013)
- **Liverpool**
  (2004 - 2010)
- **Valencia**
  (2001–2004)

## Honours

- **UEFA Champions League** (2005)
- **La Liga** (2002, 2004)
- **UEFA Europa League** (2013)
- **UEFA Cup** (2004)
- **UEFA Manager of the Year**
  (2004, 2005)
- **FA Cup** (2006)
- **Coppa Italia** (2014)
- **EFL Championship** (2017)

## Most Used Formations

- 4-2-3-1, 4-4-2, 4-3-3, 5-4-1

## Style of Play

**Steven Gerrard:** "Benítez was the best I worked with, tactically and in terms of setting up a team to win or get over the line in different situations."

"We had a very good team in the Champions League with Liverpool where we felt we could beat anyone, because we were able to adapt tactically and play like two different teams."

## Coaching Philosophy

"I am always fully focused on training and coaching my team."

"For me, knowledge is what a footballer values most from a coach. From there, you must have confidence in yourself, respect for professionals and be a worker. It is very difficult to be a winner without being a worker."

"There are players who need reinforcements immediately after a game, others the next day, others during the week, others need you to demand and press continuously. Each coach is how he is and has his own way of dealing with the motivation of the players. But in general, to win, you must be demanding and the players must understand that this requirement is for their benefit."

## What it takes to be a Successful Coach

"A good coach is a mix between knowledge and daily work."

"As a manager, you are important sometimes, and you make mistakes, but the most important people are your staff and your players. Never call me 'the special one!'"

# RAFAEL BENÍTEZ

## Interview with Rafael Benítez

# INTERVIEW WITH RAFAEL BENÍTEZ

**SOURCE:** Rafael Benítez interview conducted by Paco Cordobés and published by **abfutbol.es**

## What should an elite coach have?

**RB:** "For me, knowledge is what a footballer values most from a coach. From there, you must have confidence in yourself, respect for professionals and be a worker. It is very difficult to be a winner without being a worker."

## You are a coach who has introduced some technological elements in football. How important is managing information about your team and the opponent?

**Rafael Benítez:** "It is important to know all the information possible, because it will help you prepare your team much better. You still have the same players and tools, but if you know the weaknesses of your rival you can undoubtedly take advantage of that."

## You have been a pioneering coach when it comes to the use of data. Is it an advantage against coaches who do not use these technological advances?

**RB:** "I have always said that "the computer does not score goals but it helps to manage the information," so you can handle the information much faster, and logically you can use it to train better."

## One of the keys to your success appears to be that you're able to interpret and select data and apply it to the pitch. Is this true?

**RB:** "For me, the key is that I have always known how to surround myself with people who help me manage this information, I have always had a good team, and together we take advantage of this information.

There is so much data that can be collected, such as statistics, videos, computers that dissect strategic actions like counter attacks, etc. All that, one person cannot manage it and I say again, you need a good team of analysts to draw conclusions."

## There are many coaches who are afraid of technology, and consider that the essence of football is lost by introducing a modern tool in this sport. What do you think about this question?

**RB:** "The idea is precisely to take advantage of technology without losing the essence of football. That is the key, try to learn more about the ins and outs of the game and then give value to the most important notes.

Always check that a team is organised and observe that you have players who know how to put into practice the systems you want."

---

**Source:** Rafael Benítez interview conducted by Paco Cordobés and published by **abfutbol.es**

## Should the fitness coaches have an input in the technical and tactical training?

**RB:** "I believe that the responsibility of a professional team is so great that in the end, the head that is cut is that of the coach. I see it from my perspective. You definitely have to make decisions and you have to answer for them, and not your staff. Although you independently have full confidence in your staff. Everyone has a mission.

The other question is whether a specific coach has or doesn't have the capacity to give their opinion on technical or tactical aspects, or any other general aspect of the team. It is more a matter of trust, rather than a question of job title, because there are many people who do not have a degree and have a good vision of football for which they deserve to be heard.

Anyway, in the end you are the only one who must make the decisions. Sometimes I am left with doubts after making a mistake, wondering if I should have listened to another person before making the final decision. Therefore, my conclusion is that you have to listen to all opinions but you as the coach of the team must decide."

## You came to another football very different from Spain. When did you start to think about how to adapt to the "Liverpool" style or mark your own style?

**RB:** "The first thing to know is the characteristics of the club and their traditions. They are much more famous than other English teams and the philosophy has always been to play well, pass correctly, touch and support constantly. Then you think if you can handle it, and you can carry it out. On the other hand, you think that if you are here it is because they have signed you for what you have done, therefore you cannot change your style too much. In short, you find your own style, that mix between what you want to do and what they would like to see on the pitch."

## You won the Champions League in 2005 with a relatively low budget. How did you prepare the players from the first day to believe that they could be European champions?

**RB:** "Little by little you sow the idea that the group and the collective work is important. On top of that, you must have good players who can impact games in a big way. When you win a game like against Olympiacos when we were 1-0 down and we had to score 3 to progress, that is contagious and the team gains a lot more strength."

## How do you think you have to introduce psychological reinforcements within a team to achieve your goals?

**RB:** "I think there are no rules in this sense. There are players who need reinforcements immediately after a game, others the next day, others during the week, others need you to demand and press continuously. Each coach is how he is and has his own way of dealing with the motivation of the players. But in general, to win, you must be demanding and the player must understand that this requirement is for their benefit."

## The general concept about Rafael Benítez is that you are a coach who trusts more in a team unit rather than individuals. Is that true?

**RB:** "To win a game you need stars and to win titles you need a team. All the modest clubs have a team, but the titles are only won by clubs that have great players. There is the key, because if not, everything would be work and we would all be at the same level. What makes the difference are the good players, if they are in a good team and if they are well organised. It is difficult for a single player to win a tournament. You can win a match this way, but a competition such as the Premier League or Champions League is always won by a team."

**Source:** Rafael Benítez interview conducted by Paco Cordobés and published by **abfutbol.es**

*Del Bosque, Emery, Benítez & Luis Enrique*

# Benítez Tactical Example (Attacking): Creating Space to Exploit 2 v 1 Situation

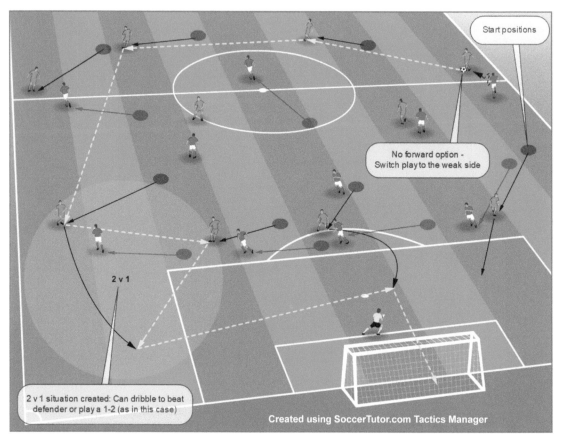

Start positions

No forward option - Switch play to the weak side

2 v 1

2 v 1 situation created: Can dribble to beat defender or play a 1-2 (as in this case)

Created using SoccerTutor.com Tactics Manager

This attacking tactical example is from Rafael Benítez's time at Liverpool. The opponents are in an organised defensive block, with the players all within their own half.

The first aim for Benítez is to switch the play and move the opposing players to create spaces.

The final aim is to create a 2 v 1 situation in the final third, which can be exploited to create a goal scoring chance.

The Liverpool left back is in possession and there is no forward passing option due to the pressing of the opposing winger. Liverpool therefore switch play along the back line and the centre back passes forward to the right winger.

Benítez's teams always look to exploit these defensive imbalances (2 v 1). The Liverpool winger can either dribble to beat the defender or play a 1-2, and then cross into the penalty area.

**Source:** Rafael Benítez's Liverpool tactics from an interview conducted by Paco Cordobés and published by **abfutbol.es**

*Del Bosque, Emery, Benítez & Luis Enrique*

# Benítez Tactical Example (Defending): Reactions when Opponents Move in Between the Lines

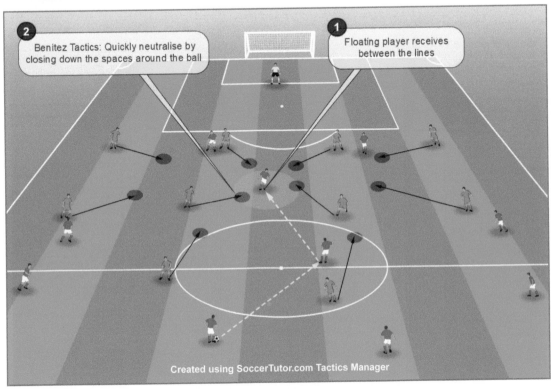

**2** Benitez Tactics: Quickly neutralise by closing down the spaces around the ball

**1** Floating player receives between the lines

Created using SoccerTutor.com Tactics Manager

This defending tactical example is from Rafael Benítez's time at Liverpool and works on combatting teams that have skilful players who float and receive between the lines, along with midfielders who can make quick forward passes.

The opponents have successfully played through the centre and there is a floating player ready to receive in between Liverpool's defensive and midfield lines.

Rafael Benítez's Liverpool team would combat this situation by marking in zones.

The Liverpool midfield and defence are compact and close together, which means there is less space available between the lines.

Once the ball is played into the floating player, all of Liverpool's players move towards the ball to condense the space.

This would stop the floating player from being able to turn, block passing lanes and limit the time and space available for him. This would often lead to Liverpool winning possession.

**Source:** Rafael Benítez's Liverpool tactics from an interview conducted by Paco Cordobés and published by **abfutbol.es**

# RAFAEL BENITEZ

## Napoli Training Session 1

*Del Bosque, Emery, Benítez & Luis Enrique*

# 1. Technical Diamond Passing Drill

**10 min**

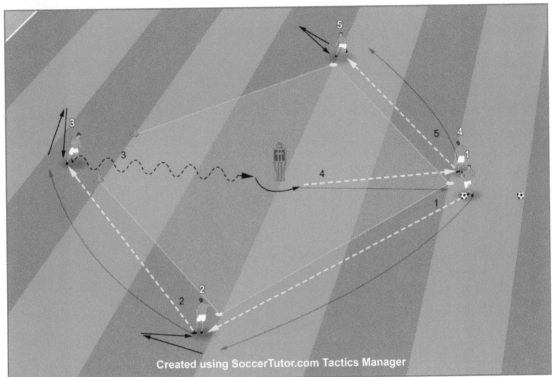

Created using SoccerTutor.com Tactics Manager

* Before this practice, the session starts with 10 minutes of stretching exercises.

**Objective:** Passing and receiving (checking away and opening up) + dribbling.

## Description

For this practice, mark out cones in a diamond shape as shown, with a mannequin in the middle.

Before each pass, the players check away from their cone and then move to receive. This is the sequence of passes and movement:

1. Player 1 passes to Player 2 and follows the pass.

2. Player 2 passes to Player 3 and follows the pass.

3. Player 3 receives, dribbles between the red cones, around the mannequin, passes to Player 4 and moves to the start position.

4. The practice then continues on the opposite side, starting with Player 4's pass to Player 5.

---

**Source:** Rafael Benítez's Napoli training session observed by **Enzo Misuraca** and published by **ForzaItalianFootball.com**

# 2. Technical Diamond Passing Drill with Quick One-Two Combinations

**10 min**

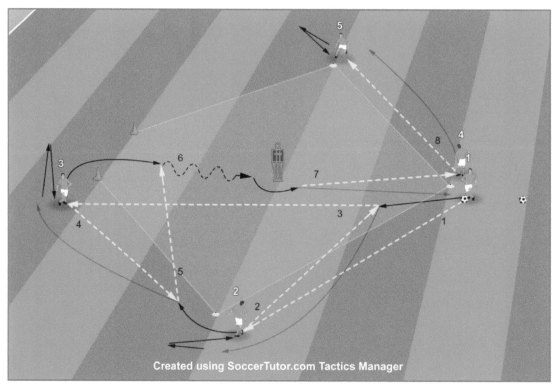

Created using SoccerTutor.com Tactics Manager

## Description

This is a progression of the previous practice. The players still check away from their cone and then move to receive.

This is the sequence of passes and movement:

1. Player 1 plays a 1-2 with Player 2 and passes to Player 3. Player 1 then moves to position 2.

2. Player 3 plays a 1-2 with Player 2, running through the cones to receive the return pass. Player 2 moves to position 3.

3. Player 3 dribbles around the mannequin, passes to Player 4 and moves to the start position.

4. The practice then continues on the opposite side, starting with Player 4's pass to Player 5.

\* After this practice, have 10 minutes of stretching exercises.

**Source:** Rafael Benítez's Napoli training session observed by **Enzo Misuraca** and published by **ForzaItalianFootball.com**

*Del Bosque, Emery, Benítez & Luis Enrique*

# 3. Technical Diamond Passing Drill with Receiving and Dribbling at Speed

**10 min**

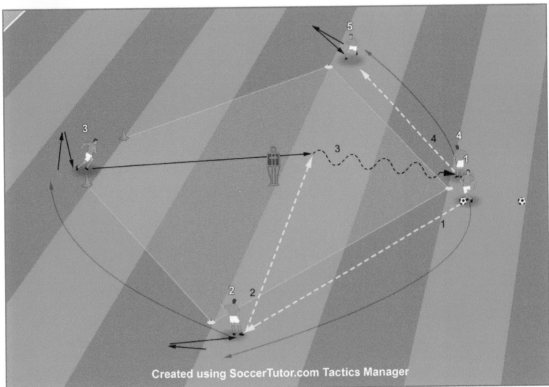

Created using SoccerTutor.com Tactics Manager

## Description

This is a variation of the previous practice. The players still check away from their cone and then move to receive.

This is the sequence of passes and movement:

1. Player 1 passes to Player 2 and follows the pass.

2. Player 2 passes in front of the mannequin and moves to position 3.

3. Player 3 has sprinted forward and timed his run to receive Player 2's pass on the move ("run in behind"). He then dribbles to the start position.

4. The practice continues on the opposite side, starting with Player 4's pass to Player 5.

**Source:** Rafael Benítez's Napoli training session observed by **Enzo Misuraca** and published by **ForzaItalianFootball.com**

*Del Bosque, Emery, Benítez & Luis Enrique*

# 4. Speed of Play and Switch in a Dynamic 4 Zone Rondo

**10 min**

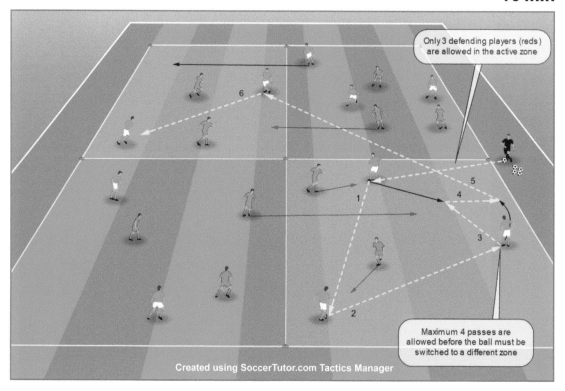

Only 3 defending players (reds) are allowed in the active zone

Maximum 4 passes are allowed before the ball must be switched to a different zone

Created using SoccerTutor.com Tactics Manager

**Objective:** Quick passing and fast ball circulation to quickly switch the point of attack.

## Description

In a 20 x 20 yard area, the players can move freely across the 4 zones but only 3 players from the defending team are allowed in the active zone (where the ball is) at one time.

The practice starts with the coach's pass to one of the teams (blues in diagram). The blue team aim to maintain possession.

**Rule:** A maximum of 4 passes can be played within a zone before the ball must be switched into a different zone. This forces the players to keep the ball moving quickly and constantly switch the play.

The red defending team work together to try and win the ball. If they do, they then have the same aim to maintain possession across the 4 zones and the blues try to win the ball back.

\* After this practice, have 10 minutes of strength exercises (abdominal crunches, press-ups and triceps).

**Source:** Rafael Benítez's Napoli training session observed by **Enzo Misuraca** and published by **ForzaItalianFootball.com**

*Del Bosque, Emery, Benítez & Luis Enrique*

## 5. Build Up to Finish in a Conditioned Game with Passing Gates

**20 min**

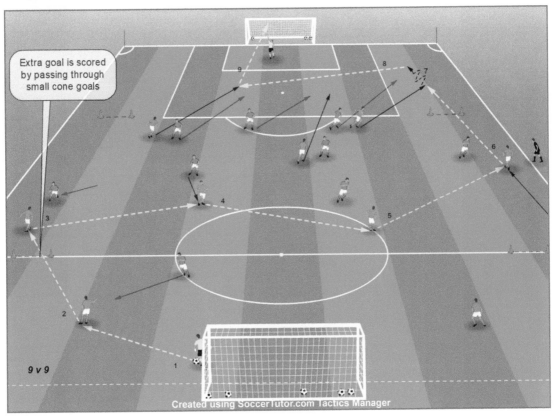

Extra goal is scored by passing through small cone goals

9 v 9

Created using SoccerTutor.com Tactics Manager

**Objective:** Team shape, build up play, accurate passing and finishing attacks.

### Description

We play a normal 9 v 9 game (10 v 10 with GKs), except there are 4 cone gates in the positions shown.

The practice starts from the goalkeeper and the blue team must build up play within their set formation and team shape. The ultimate aim is to play the ball forward and score a goal (1 point).

However, the blue team can also score 1 point by passing through any cone gate.

The players have to use correct and intelligent movement to create passing lines and demonstrate accurate driven passes along the ground.

* After this practice, do a cool down for 10 minutes.

**Source:** Rafael Benítez's Napoli training session observed by **Enzo Misuraca** and published by **ForzaItalianFootball.com**

*Del Bosque, Emery, Benítez & Luis Enrique*

# RAFAEL BENITEZ

## Napoli Training Session 2

*Del Bosque, Emery, Benítez & Luis Enrique*

# 1. Open Up to Receive, One-Two + Long Pass in a Technical Passing Sequence

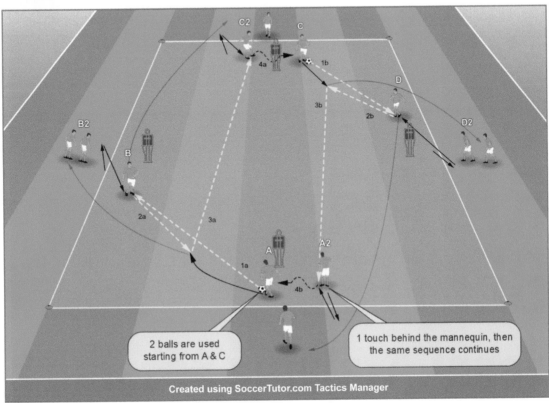

2 balls are used starting from A & C

1 touch behind the mannequin, then the same sequence continues

Created using SoccerTutor.com Tactics Manager

**Objective:** A drill frequently used by Rafael Benítez to improve passing and receiving techniques.

## Description

In an 18-20 yard x 25 yard area, there are a minimum of 6 players. Play with 2 balls simultaneously from A and C. Before each pass, players check away and then move to receive. This is the sequence:

1. A plays a 1-2 combination with B and passes to C2.
   C plays a 1-2 combination with D and passes to A2.

2. C2 opens up and takes a first touch behind the mannequin.
   A2 opens up and takes a first touch behind the mannequin.

3. A2 and C2 restart the same sequence by playing 1-2 combinations with B2 and D2 respectively.

4. All players move to the next position (A -> B -> C -> D -> A).

**Source:** Rafael Benítez's Napoli training session observed by **Massimo Lucchesi** and published on **NewSoccerDrills.com**

*Del Bosque, Emery, Benítez & Luis Enrique*

# 2. Technical One-Touch Pass and Move Combination

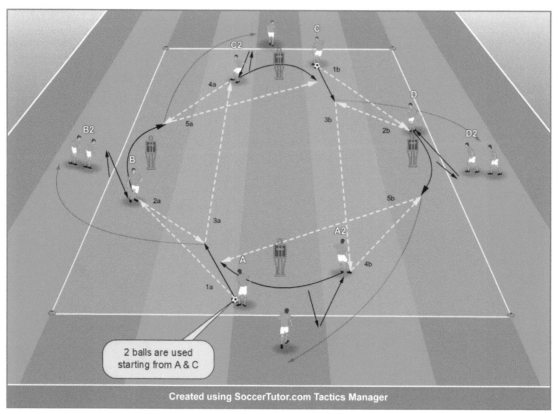

2 balls are used starting from A & C

Created using SoccerTutor.com Tactics Manager

## Description

This is a progression of the previous practice. Play again with 2 balls simultaneously from A and C. Before each pass, the players check away and then move to receive. This is the sequence of passes:

1. A plays a 1-2 combination with B and passes to C2.
   C plays a 1-2 combination with D and passes to A2.

2. C2 plays a 1-2 combination with B and runs behind the mannequin to receive the return pass.
   A2 plays a 1-2 combination with D and runs behind the mannequin to receive the return pass.

3. A2 and C2 restart the same sequence by playing 1-2 combinations with B2 and D2 respectively.

4. All players move to the next position (A -> B -> C -> D -> A).

---

**Source:** Rafael Benítez's Napoli training session observed by **Massimo Lucchesi** and published on **NewSoccerDrills.com**

*Del Bosque, Emery, Benítez & Luis Enrique*

# 3. Switching Play and Quick Support in a 7 v 3 Possession Game

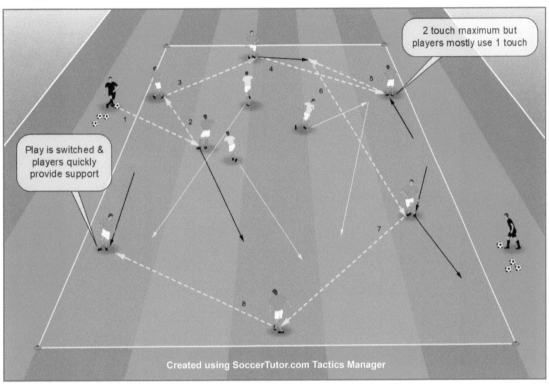

**Objective:** Passing, receiving, intercepting and transitions.

## Description

In a 10 x 20 yard area, we play a 7 v 3 possession game. The blue team have 6 players who are positioned on the outsides and 1 player who operates in the middle.

The practice starts with the coach's pass to the blue team who aim to keep possession. The players are limited to 2 touches but should look to mainly use 1 touch.

The blue team should keep looking to switch the play from one end to the other and then quickly provide support for the player in possession.

The other 3 players (wearing yellow bibs) work together on the inside and try to win the ball. When one of the 3 yellow players intercepts a pass, he switches position with the blue player that gave the ball away.

**Source:** Rafael Benítez's Napoli training session observed by **Massimo Lucchesi** and published on **NewSoccerDrills.com**

*Del Bosque, Emery, Benítez & Luis Enrique*

# 4. Passing Through the Lines in a Tactical Practice with Receiving Zones

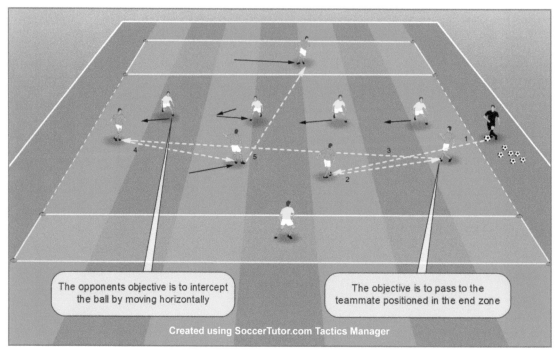

The opponents objective is to intercept the ball by moving horizontally

The objective is to pass to the teammate positioned in the end zone

Created using SoccerTutor.com Tactics Manager

**Attacking Objective:** Passing through the lines, creating passing angles and accurate passing.

**Defending Objective:** Keeping compact, communication, blocking passing angles and anticipation to intercept.

## Description

In an 18 x 25 yard area, we mark out 2 end zones (5 yards). Both teams have 4 players inside the main area and 1 extra player in an end zone.

The practice starts with the coach's pass to a blue player. The blue team move the ball between each other, waiting for the right time to pass the ball to their teammate in the end zone (1 point).

The player in the end zone should be constantly moving to create a passing line to receive.

The yellow team work together, keeping close distances between each other and trying to intercept any attempted passes.

Whether the pass is successful or not, the coach plays a new ball into the yellow team and the practice continues with the same aims in the opposite direction.

**Source:** Rafael Benítez's Napoli training session observed by **Massimo Lucchesi** and published on **NewSoccerDrills.com**

# 5. 3 Team Possession Game with Outside "Rebound Players"

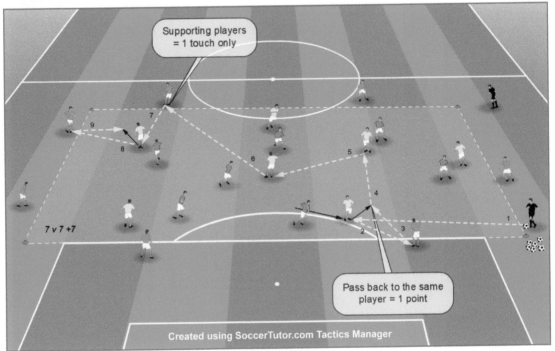

**Objective:** This Rafael Benítez's practice focuses on developing many skills such as passing, receiving, intercepting the ball and pressing.

## Description

Two teams (red and yellow) play 7 v 7 inside the area and we have a third team (blue) that are positioned outside as shown, and play with the team in possession of the ball.

The practice starts with the coach's pass to the yellow team - the yellows and blues try to maintain possession of the ball. The red defending team work together to try and win the ball.

The blue outside players are limited to 1 touch.

The yellow team score 1 point if a player passes to an outside player (blue) and receives a "rebound pass" (1 touch) back successfully.

Keep changing the team roles throughout the practice.

**Source:** Rafael Benítez's Napoli training session observed by **Massimo Lucchesi** and published on **NewSoccerDrills.com**

# LUIS ENRIQUE

**This section includes:**

- Luis Enrique's FC Barcelona: A Tactical Analysis
- 1 Full Roma Training Session (10 Practices)
- 4 FC Barcelona Practices

# LUIS ENRIQUE

*"Our goal is to play the same, looking for goals, whatever the result."*

## Coaching Roles

- **Spain**
  (2018 - Present)
- **FC Barcelona**
  (2014 - 2017)
- **Celta Vigo**
  (2013 - 2014)
- **Roma**
  (2011 - 2012)
- **Barcelona B**
  (2008 - 2011)

## Honours

- **UEFA Champions League**
  (2015)
- **La Liga**
  (2015, 2016)
- **Copa del Rey**
  (2015, 2016, 2017)
- **FIFA Club World Cup**
  (2015)
- **FIFA World Coach of the Year**
  (2015)

## Most Used Formation

- **4-3-3**

## Style of Play

"Our goal is to play the same, looking for goals, whatever the result. Sometimes it's interesting to have a different type of game, but always controlling the play. If the opponent pressures us then more space appears, to know what areas of the pitch you can do more damage to the rival in is key."

"We will try to keep the ball as we always do, as long as we can throughout the game."

## Coaching Philosophy

"If I didn't feel that I was helping my team and my players, and didn't feel that very clearly, then I wouldn't be coaching."

"When we came to Barça, one of our first targets was to make the team less predictable. That's not easy with a team that plays for possession. But Barça have many other resources to draw on now."

## What it takes to be a Successful Coach

"Coaches never enjoy anything. In football you can't live in the past or the future, only the present, and that is the next game. Only when you finish the season and you have achieved your objectives can you enjoy it, but not for long."

# LUIS ENRIQUE

## FC Barcelona: A Tactical Analysis

# Luis Enrique's Tactics in the Champions League vs Paris Saint-Germain

**Paris Saint-Germain 1-3 Barcelona** (Champions League Quarter Final 1st Leg, 15th April 2015)

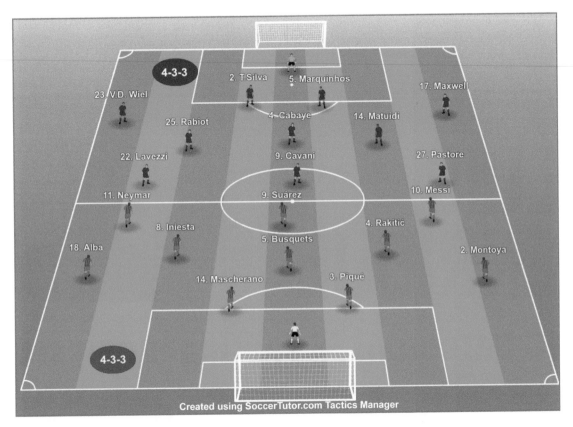

Barcelona played a 4-3-3 formation in this Champions League quarter final, as they did the majority of the time under Luis Enrique.

Enrique's tactical approach was more conservative than usual, as not all 3 forwards stayed high up the pitch. **Neymar** tracked PSG's right back V. D. Wiel on the left.

The striker **Suárez** was always positioned between the 2 centre backs T. Silva and Marquinhos, while the right winger **Messi** would most often leave the PSG left back Maxwell

unmarked and move towards the centre to create a 2 v 2 situation against the PSG centre backs.

Barcelona looked to dominate the ball with **Busquets** (defensive midfielder), **Iniesta** and **Rakitić** all getting plenty of touches and combining with the front 3.

Barça played with a back 4, with the emphasis on the left back **Jordi Alba** to attack, combine with **Iniesta** and **Neymar**, and move into advanced areas to receive in space.

---

**Source:** Luis Enrique's Barcelona vs PSG - Tactical analysis by **Terzis Athanasios**, published by **SoccerTeamTactics.com**

98

# Luis Enrique's Attacking Combination Play on the Flank

## 2 Player Combination to Create Space for the Full Back High Up on the Flank

Created using SoccerTutor.com Tactics Manager

During the attacking phase, Barcelona tried to dominate possession and dictate the tempo.

However, they couldn't be creative through the centre as the PSG players restricted the space available. Their success in this game came from many attacking combinations on the left side. This was also partly due to exposing an apparent weakness in the PSG right back V. D. Wiel (23).

Barcelona's right back **Montoya (2)** didn't seem very comfortable when moving forward, so Barça took advantage of the strength on their left side with **Alba (18)**, **Iniesta (8)** and **Neymar (11)** using quick and quality combination play to take advantage of the available space out wide.

This example shows the defensive midfielder **Busquets (5)** passing to the left back **Alba (18)**.

**Alba (18)** passes out wide to **Neymar (11)** on the side-line and this draws in both the right winger Lavezzi (22) and right back V. D. Wiel (23), which creates space in behind him.

**Neymar (11)** passes forward to **Alba (18)**, who makes a fast run forward to receive in the created space (1-2 combination). **Alba (18)** received in this position many times during the game, and would try and create goal scoring opportunities. In this example, he tries a cross to **Suárez (9)**, but it is blocked by PSG centre back Marquinhos (5).

**Source:** Luis Enrique's Barcelona vs PSG - Tactical analysis by **Terzis Athanasios**, published by **SoccerTeamTactics.com**

*Del Bosque, Emery, Benítez & Luis Enrique*

## 3 Player Combination to Create Space for the Full Back High Up on the Flank

Created using SoccerTutor.com Tactics Manager

In this variation of the previous tactical example, Barcelona now use a 3 player combination to create space for their left back **Jordi Alba (18)** to receive free in space high up the pitch.

In contrast to the previous example, the left winger **Neymar (11)** is positioned more inside and has dropped back, while the left back **Alba (18)** is positioned out wide on the side-line.

The defensive midfielder **Busquets (5)** is in possession again, but this time he passes to **Neymar (11)**.

At the same time that **Neymar (11)** drops off, the central midfielder **Iniesta (8)** moves forward and is left unmarked. This synchronised movement was seen a lot in Luis Enrique's Barcelona team and enabled them to break through the opposition's midfield line to progress attacks.

**Neymar (11)** acts as the link player and passes first time to **Iniesta (8)**.

Barcelona have now successfully received between the midfield and defensive lines of their opponents PSG.

The PSG right back V. D. Wiel (23) is drawn to **Iniesta (8)**, so **Iniesta** plays a pass out wide into the available space for the left back **Jordi Alba (18)** to run onto and dribble forward into a dangerous area in behind the opposition's defensive line.

As explained on the previous page, **Alba (18)** received in this position many times during the game, and would then create goal scoring opportunities.

**Source:** Luis Enrique's Barcelona vs PSG - Tactical analysis by **Terzis Athanasios**, published by **SoccerTeamTactics.com**

# Attack with a Third Man Run to Receive in Behind a Deep Defensive Line

## Full Back Makes a Third Man Run to Receive in the Box After an Inside Pass

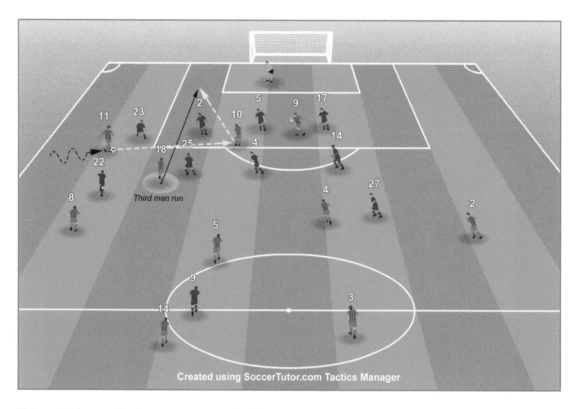

Created using SoccerTutor.com Tactics Manager

This tactical example shows one way in which Luis Enrique would try to attack against a deep defensive line.

As shown, PSG are in a compact 4-4 defensive formation deep within their own half and **Neymar (11)** has the ball at his feet high up on the left flank.

From this position, Luis Enrique's Barcelona team would look to play quick combinations to receive in behind and in the penalty area. They would often use a third man run from a deeper player, as shown in this tactical example with the left back Jordi **Alba (18)**.

**Neymar (11)** dribbles inside and passes to **Messi (10)**, who is very comfortable in tight spaces.

As soon as **Neymar (11)** makes the pass, **Alba (18)** makes a forward run into the box. **Messi (10)** passes in behind for **Alba (18)** and Barça are in a very dangerous position.

This kind of third man run was a popular tactic against deep defences during Luis Enrique's time at Barcelona.

---

**Source:** Luis Enrique's Barcelona vs PSG - Tactical analysis by **Terzis Athanasios**, published by **SoccerTeamTactics.com**

# Luis Enrique's Counter Attack Tactics

## Fast Break Attack with Quick Combination Play to Exploit Space in Behind

When Barcelona won the ball off PSG in this match, they would often find their opponents to be unbalanced.

In this tactical example, the defensive midfielder **Busquets (5)** wins the ball near the left flank on the halfway line. <u>PSG's midfield and defence are disorganised, so Barcelona are able to capitalise with a fast break attack</u>. PSG centre back Marquinhos (5) is out of position, with Cabaye (4) in a deep position to provide cover.

**Busquets (5)** wins the ball and plays quickly forward to **Rakitić (4)**. The PSG right back V. D.

Wiel (23) decides to move forward and contest him. This reaction unbalances PSG, so when **Messi (10)** receives the pass from **Rakitić (4)**, a 3 v 2 situation is created.

**Messi (10)** passes at the right time to **Neymar (11)** in the space created - **Neymar** controls the ball, moves inside and scores.

Barcelona took advantage of the positive transition to score the opening goal (18 min) when the match seemed balanced, despite Barça's domination of possession.

---

**Source:** Luis Enrique's Barcelona vs PSG - Tactical analysis by **Terzis Athanasios**, published by **SoccerTeamTactics.com**

# LUIS ENRIQUE

# Roma Training Session

*Del Bosque, Emery, Benítez & Luis Enrique*

# 1. Maintaining Possession in Tight Spaces in a 5 v 3 Rondo

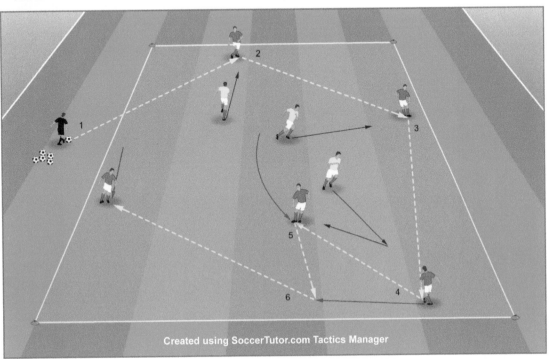

Created using SoccerTutor.com Tactics Manager

**Objective:** Keeping possession in tight spaces.

## Description

In a 15 x 18 yard area, the red team have 4 players along the outsides (1 on each side of the rectangle) and 1 player inside. The yellow team have their 3 players all inside.

The practice starts with the coach's pass to the red team, who aim to keep possession against their 3 yellow opponents.

The yellow team work together to press and try to win the ball. If a yellow player wins the ball, he switches roles with the outside player who lost it.

## Coaching Points

1. The players need to play precise passes (accurate and well-weighted).
2. The key to this practice is spatial awareness, utilising all of the limited space available.
3. It is very important that the player in possession of the ball makes fast and effective choices to find a free teammate and pass him the ball.

**Source:** Luis Enrique's Roma training session observed by **Massimo Lucchesi** and published on **NewSoccerDrills.com**

*Del Bosque, Emery, Benítez & Luis Enrique*

# 2. Playing Through the Opposition and Fast Transitions in a 6 v 6 (+1) Tactical Practice with Mini Goals

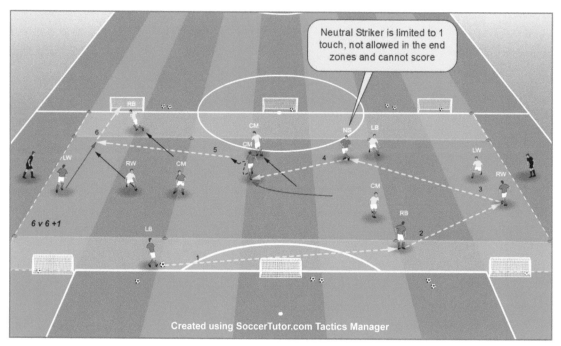

Neutral Striker is limited to 1 touch, not allowed in the end zones and cannot score

*Created using SoccerTutor.com Tactics Manager*

**Attacking Objective:** Playing through the opposition to move into the final stage of attack.

**Defending Objective:** Recovering the ball and effective transitions from defence to attack.

## Description

Each team has 6 players with 2 full backs (LB & RB), 2 wingers (LW & RW) and 2 central midfielders (CM). There is also 1 blue neutral player (NS) who plays with the team in possession as a striker.

The practice starts with a full back (LB in diagram) and the red team build up play, utilising the neutral striker to try and play through their opponents and score in one of the mini goals. The neutral striker (NS) is not allowed to enter the end zone or score a goal.

The yellow defending team work collectively to try and win the ball. If they do, they then make a fast transition to attack and try to score in the mini goals at the other end. The red team must make a fast transition from attack to defence and prevent the yellows from scoring.

**Rules for Defending Team:** Each full back can only defend 1 goal. The left back (LB) defends the goal on the left and the right back (RB) defends the goal on the right. The central midfielders (CM) defend the middle goal.

---

**Source:** Luis Enrique's Roma training session observed by **Massimo Lucchesi** and published on **NewSoccerDrills.com**

# 3. Attacking Patterns of Play and Finishing in an 8 v 5 Tactical Game

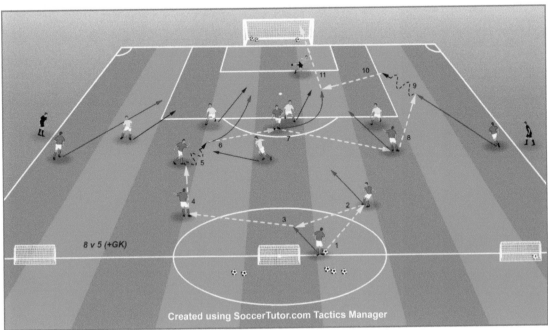

8 v 5 (+GK)

Created using SoccerTutor.com Tactics Manager

**Attacking Objective:** Attacking patterns of play and enhancing the effectiveness of finishing attacks.

**Defending Objective:** The defending team works on keeping compact and defending the goal, pressing and improving their ball recovery skills.

## Description

The red attacking team have 8 players: 2 full backs, 3 central midfielders, 2 wingers and 1 forward. The practice starts with the defensive midfielder and their aim is to use attacking patterns of play (different combinations), take advantage of their numerical superiority and try to score.

In the diagram example, the red team use their advanced full backs and exploit the space out wide to create a chance and score.

The yellow defending team have 5 players: 2 centre backs, 2 full backs and 1 defensive midfielder. Their aim is to defend the goal and work together to intercept/recover the ball.

If the yellows win the ball, they launch a counter attack and try to pass into one of the mini goals on the halfway line. These goals represent 2 wingers and 1 forward, who would look to receive in a real match situation.

---

**Source:** Luis Enrique's Roma training session observed by **Massimo Lucchesi** and published on **NewSoccerDrills.com**

*Del Bosque, Emery, Benítez & Luis Enrique*

# 4. Exploiting a Numerical Advantage to Finish in Continuous 3 v 2 Duels

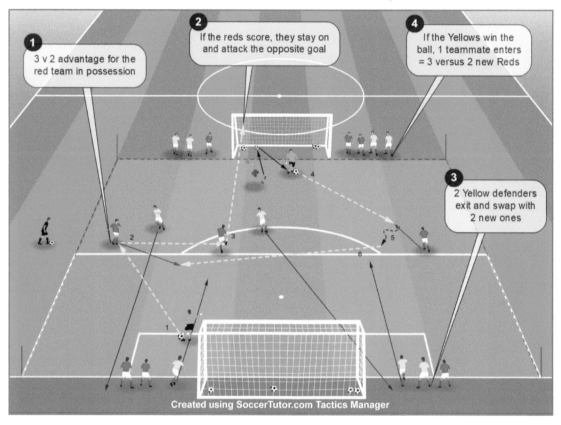

**1** 3 v 2 advantage for the red team in possession

**2** If the reds score, they stay on and attack the opposite goal

**4** If the Yellows win the ball, 1 teammate enters = 3 versus 2 new Reds

**3** 2 Yellow defenders exit and swap with 2 new ones

Created using SoccerTutor.com Tactics Manager

**Attacking Objective:** Exploiting a numerical advantage and finishing.

**Defending Objective:** Pressing and winning the ball.

## Description

In an area double the size of the penalty box, we have 2 goalkeepers defending 2 full-size goals.

1. The practice starts with the goalkeeper and a 3 v 2 duel, with the reds trying to score.

2. If the red team score, they stay inside the area and attack the other goal.

3. The reds attack against 2 new defenders (2 yellow defenders exit and swap with 2 new ones).

4. If the 2 yellow defenders win the ball at any time, 1 extra yellow player enters and they become the attacking team. They will attack in a 3 v 2 duel against 2 new red defenders (the 3 red players who lost possession exit the grid and swap with 2 new red players).

**Source:** Luis Enrique's Roma training session observed by **Massimo Lucchesi** and published on **NewSoccerDrills.com**

# 5. Various Tactical Situations in a Dynamic 3 Team Zonal Practice

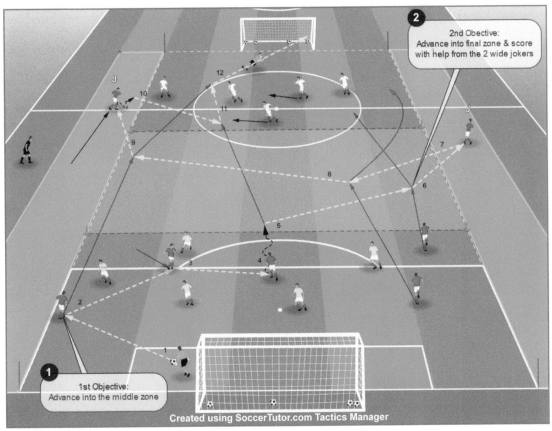

**Objective:** Playing in tight spaces to work on various tactical situations at the same time (build up, moving into the final stage of attack, finishing and transitions).

## Description

1. The practice starts with the red team's goalkeeper and a 5 v 5 situation against the yellow team in Zone 1. The reds can either dribble or pass into Zone 2 (middle zone).

2. When in Zone 2, the reds use the 2 blue jokers (in side zones) and attack the white team in Zone 3. With the help of the jokers, the reds have a 7 v 5 numerical advantage to finish their attack.

3. If the yellows win the ball in Zone 1, the team roles are reversed, so the yellows look to play into Zone 2 (middle zone) and then attack the whites in Zone 3. The reds stay in Zone 1.

4. If the whites win the ball in Zone 3, the team roles are reversed, so they look to play into Zone 2 and then attack the yellows in Zone 1. The reds stay in Zone 3.

**Source:** Luis Enrique's Roma training session observed by **Massimo Lucchesi** and published on **NewSoccerDrills.com**

*Del Bosque, Emery, Benítez & Luis Enrique*

# LUIS ENRIQUE

## FC Barcelona Training Practices

*Del Bosque, Emery, Benítez & Luis Enrique*

# 1. Positional 4 v 4 (+3) Rondo with Fast Transitions

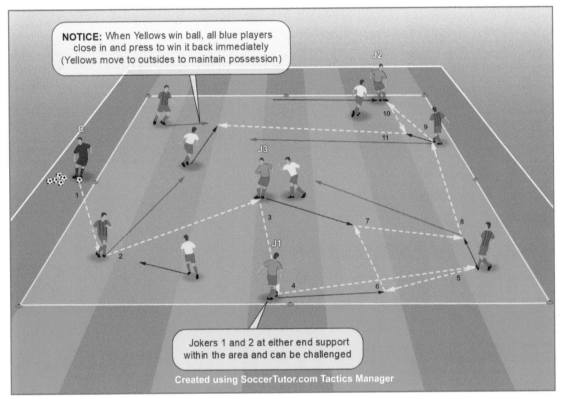

NOTICE: When Yellows win ball, all blue players close in and press to win it back immediately (Yellows move to outsides to maintain possession)

Jokers 1 and 2 at either end support within the area and can be challenged

Created using SoccerTutor.com Tactics Manager

**Objective:** Maintaining possession + fast defensive transition to recover ball as quickly as possible.

## Description

In a 15 yard square, we have 2 teams of 4 (blue and yellow) + 3 red jokers who play with the team in possession. All 4 blue players are positioned on the sides (2 on each side) and all the yellow players play inside the area. There is also 1 red joker at each end (J1 and J2) and 1 inside (J3).

The practice starts with the coach and the blue team try to maintain possession with help from the 3 red jokers. The yellow team work together (pressing) and try to win the ball.

If the ball goes out of play, the practice continues with a new ball and the blues still in possession.

If the yellows are able to intercept the ball, the teams switch roles and all of the blue players immediately close in and press the ball carrier to try and win the ball back immediately. The yellows move to the outsides and try to maintain possession.

**Source:** Luis Enrique's Barcelona training session at Mini Estadi, Barcelona - 4th January 2016

*Del Bosque, Emery, Benítez & Luis Enrique*

# 2. Switching Play in a Dynamic 3 Team Rondo and Transition Game

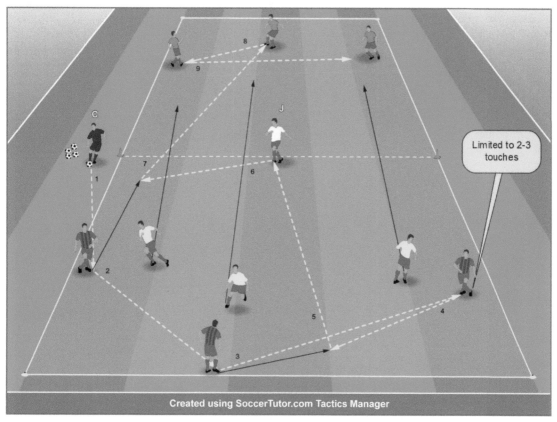

Limited to 2-3 touches

Created using SoccerTutor.com Tactics Manager

**Attacking Objective:** Creating space and angles to maintain possession and switch the play + support play and fast transitions to defence after losing the ball.

**Defending Objective:** Collective pressing, communication, anticipation and interceptions.

## Description

In a 12 x 36 yard area, we have 3 teams of 3 (blues, yellows and reds) + 1 joker on the halfway line. We start with blues vs yellows in one half. The team in possession (blues in diagram) are limited to 2-3 touches and must maintain possession, with the aim to pass to the joker (J). The joker passes the ball back to a blue player, who then passes to a red player on the other side.

From this point, the 3 yellow players move across to defend again. The practice continues with the reds trying to switch play back to the blues via the joker. If the defending team (yellows in diagram) win the ball, they play to the other side and switch roles with the team that lost the ball.

**Source:** Luis Enrique's Barcelona training session at Mini Estadi, Barcelona - 4th January 2016

*Del Bosque, Emery, Benítez & Luis Enrique*

# 3. Fast Attacks in a 5 v 5 (+1) Small Sided Game

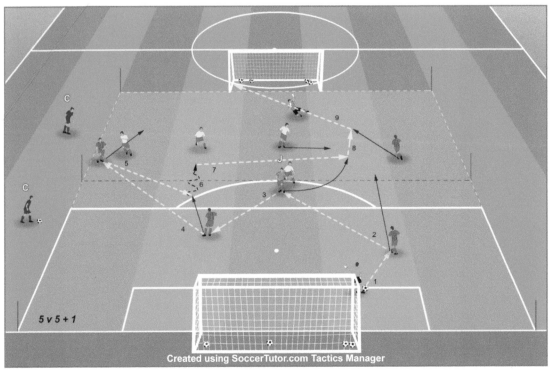

5 v 5 + 1

Created using SoccerTutor.com Tactics Manager

**Objective:** Fast attacks with support play and shooting/finishing.

## Description

In the area shown, the 2 teams play a normal 5 v 5 game +1 joker who plays with the team in possession. The emphasis of this practice is to play forward quickly and score as soon as possible.

The practice starts with the goalkeeper and he can distribute the ball in different ways (short, medium or long) - he chooses the best option to help his team score as soon as possible.

When the ball is played into the opposition's half, all the outfield players run forward to support the attack.

If the ball goes out at the sides, restart with a throw-in and if it goes out at the ends, restart from the goalkeeper.

**Source:** Luis Enrique's Barcelona training session at Mini Estadi, Barcelona - 4th January 2016

*Del Bosque, Emery, Benítez & Luis Enrique*

# 4. Positional Attacks to Play in Behind in a Dynamic Zonal Practice

**Attacking Objective:** Positional build-up play and attacks, passing and receiving in space, playing in behind the defensive line and fast defensive transitions to win the ball back after losing it.

**Defending Objective:** Collective pressing, blocking passing lines, disrupting the opposition's attack to prevent them playing in behind and fast counter attacks after winning the ball.

## Description

The blues are in a 4-3-3 formation and the yellows are in a 4-4-1 formation. The practice starts with the Coach who passes to a one of the blue centre backs in Zone 1 (2 v 1). The blues use positional attacks and try to play the ball in behind (into the penalty area). This can be done by dribbling across the line or by receiving a pass from any player in any zone.

One player can move from Zone 2 to Zone 3 to create a 3 (+1) v 4 situation, as shown with No.10 dribbling forward in the diagram example. All yellow defending players must stay within their zones, but if they win the ball, they launch a counter attack and try to play in behind at the other end.

**Source:** Luis Enrique's Barcelona training session in Tbilisi before UEFA Super Cup vs Sevilla - 11th August 2015

*Del Bosque, Emery, Benítez & Luis Enrique*

CPSIA information can be obtained
at www.ICGtesting.com
Printed in the USA
BVHW021946180419
545950BV00018B/66/P